IS ANYBODY THERE?

IS ANYBODY THERE?

EXPLORING THE UNEXPLAINED

Ghostly trails throughout England and Beyond.

by
Julie Taylor

YOUCAXTON
PUBLICATIONS

ISBN 978-1-913425-74-6

Published by YouCaxton Publications 2021
YCBN: 01

YouCaxton Publications
www.youcaxton.co.uk

My thanks go to so many who have helped with the production and publication of this book.

Russ, my very patient husband (the writer's widower).

Mo McDaid, final proof reader & editor.

Mike Willmott, proof reader.

Mary Dingley and Roger Hoult, proof readers.

Pete Legg National Trust Guide.

Martin Wood Shrewsbury Town Crier.

Gilly Pickup Writer.

The Prince Rupert Hotel.

Lilliput Doll and Toy Museum.

Geraldine Charles Royal Museums Greenwich.

Mary Evans picture gallery.

Allan Frost. My publishing mentor!

Sarah Hayes. Manager of The Coffin Works.

Philip Davies

Marcus Clayton

Olivia Flemming Smith

This book is dedicated to Mo McDaid.

Spitbank Fort
Courtesy of Russ Taylor

Contents

INTRODUCTION

MY INTENTION IS not to saturate you, the reader, with masses of history in relation to the places we are to visit, or to give an in-depth background story to the ghosts themselves. It is more to bring to the readers' attention those places that are said to be haunted, in an entertaining, yet still informative way. Hopefully, the book will be of use to those 'would-be' ghost-hunting parties, and likewise to the more cowardly - such as me - keener to avoid the more unfriendly ones at least!

The following compilation of true stories, composed by way of a ghost tour, was inspired by a visit to a hotel situated in Corfe Castle village on the Isle of Purbeck in Dorset. The hotel was a most beautiful period building. It had an immediate and unexpected impact upon me. As soon as I saw it, I knew that it was haunted - I should add - not in a good way. I am not normally inclined to make such a sweeping statement, but my experience led me to think that others might wish to be forewarned, and so I posted a review on *TripAdvisor*:

'If sensitive to the spirit world, read on...'

I will say firstly that it is not my intention to deter you from staying there, but if others had experienced the same sense of unease as I did in a part of the hotel, I would have liked to have known in advance. When I later raised the subject at Reception, my feelings were confirmed to be 100% accurate.

If you are not a believer in the afterlife, or even if you are, deciding to stay there may not bother you. If I, however, knew about the experiences of previous guests, I would certainly be hesitant, veering towards, "I don't think so".

We visited for lunch, which was excellent (hence 5 stars) - as was the service.

Within six days the review had a massive number of 'hits', and helpful votes. The hotel manager, having failed to respond to previous detrimental reviews of the hotel, responded immediately to mine:

"We're pleased you enjoyed your stay with us, particularly the food. I can say that having been here for 13 years, we have never experienced any 'spirit' encounters. I can only think that our staff thought you might have been referring to perhaps another type of spirit, namely, whisky, vodka or gin. We look forward to welcoming

you back at some point!" The Shakespearean line, '*She doth protest too much, methinks,*' immediately came to mind.

Since then, I have happened upon reviews from other people, regarding different establishments, also expressing the opinion that prospective guests may appreciate advance warning of phantom presences. Having researched the subject further, I find accounts of hauntings in public places to be numerous, to say the least! Neither is it only buildings that are haunted, but items found within them too!

I do hope you enjoy our trip, as we embark on our ghost tour together. One really does not know what awaits in the most bizarre of places!

Julie Taylor January 2020

1

SPITBANK FORT

Spitbank Fort Courtesy of Russ Taylor

MY HUSBAND, MYSELF, and two friends, Niki and Bob, visited Spitbank Fort in 2014. A rotund fort built of granite and iron, erected in the Victorian era, it is located in the middle of the Solent, Portsmouth. It cost £167,300 to build - work started in 1867, and it was finally completed in 1878.

We didn't know on booking our one-night stay that it was haunted – and, furthermore, that a whole episode had been devoted to it by the '*Britain's Most Haunted*' investigation team. Included in the one-night stay is an historical tour of the fort, and its labyrinth of tunnels and rooms.

Once you have been safely deposited on the Fort, by means of a ferry, you are there for the duration - there is no going back! Having discovered all of this, an episode from the popular '*Scooby Doo*' cartoon series came to mind. I imagined the four of us walking the dark passageways below - the braver - Russ and Niki, striding out, Bob and I, tiptoeing behind, for fear of upsetting the resident poltergeist.

Having driven in our 'Mystery Machine' to the Fort's terminal lounge at Gosport (minus Scooby), ready as we would ever be, we set sail for this unique hotel experience, and I, despite being in possession of a crucifix, blessed by holy water from Durham Cathedral, was dreading it!

It is an exclusive hotel, at times costing upward of £800 for a one-night stay. Hosting only sixteen guests, it could be likened to a scene plucked out of an Agatha Christie novel. The hotel has eight bedrooms, all superbly furnished. It is a truly luxurious experience, with excellent food and wonderful staff - many having made the acquaintance of its poltergeist, and being quite happy to relate encounters.

Henry is not the most amiable of ghosts: he had suffered a somewhat undignified ending, whereby he was blown backwards by an explosion, into the fort's well. I chuckle as I type. The image is rather like an excerpt from an episode of '*Dad's Army*'. However, it was not funny, as he was killed in the fall. His body was recovered from the well. Henry is said to be prone to violent outbursts, and being unpredictable - the words of witnesses, not mine. He blows on visitors' necks, and hisses in ears, as guests explore the myriad tunnels within the fort.

The perimeter passageway, without any means of lighting, can only be explored in absolute darkness. It probably won't come as any surprise to know, Bob and I, gave that leg of the tour a miss. Opting instead to sit outside in a small sunlit vestibule, both of us were blissfully unaware that this was one of Henry's favourite 'hot spots' for a little fun with the guests.

Our encounter with Henry (if it was him?) transpired somewhat differently. I have reviewed the event on *TripAdvisor*, and ask anyone experiencing anything in *The Cunningham Suite* to report any occurrence out of the ordinary, or inexplicable. It is the third room as one enters the residential wing. The housekeeper had told us she always felt she was being watched when working in this room: she felt as if she was never totally alone. Of course, other things may have happened elsewhere - who knows?

We thought no more of it. Having inspected the rooms and unpacked, we left. On our return, things had changed. A book and a glass, not in the room beforehand, had now appeared, placed by the window. The housekeeper agreed they had not been there when she prepared the room; further, she added that hotel staff are not permitted to enter rooms, once guests are in residence. My friend, braver than I, was a little disturbed by the incident, but not all of a quiver (as I would have been) at the thought of the night ahead. That said - come bedtime, she was a little more unnerved - asking if there was anything they could do which might dissuade Henry from paying them a 'nocturnal visit'. A little lost as to what to say, and reluctant to lend out my crucifix, having read somewhere that witches will not cross water, my only suggestion was to leave the bedroom window open. Perhaps the sound of the sea might put him off? I was later to discover, this was just about the worst advice I could have given them, as ghosts, as an energy force themselves, gain strength from the power of water! In my defence, their answer to this suggestion was that they had no choice but to do just that, for both Niki and Bob had tried to shut the bedroom window earlier, and had been unable to. Manufactured by the Victorians, it was made of extremely heavy iron.

At 3 a.m., on a perfectly still and tranquil night, both friends suddenly woke. Glancing in tandem at the window, they witnessed that same window move from its 90-degree open angle, not to slam, but instead to shut, at a slow, yet quite deliberate speed. Being the hot night that it was, they tried to open it again. No amount of force would shift it. Make of it what you will!

The fort was, to me, intimidating, menacing - those dark passageways, daunting. One never knew what might lie in wait around the next bend. I tried not to let my imagination run riot. I think I failed!

As we left on the ferry, I looked back at this imposing building, glad to be gone. Would I return? A resounding no! I am sure a large percentage would indeed carry on and go there. Furthermore – I am sure they will have a thrilling stay, one way or another at least.

As at September 2020, both Spitbank and her sister fort, *No Man's Fort* (another hotel complex located in the Solent) are both up for sale.

2

FAN BAY DEEP TUNNELS, DOVER

Fan Bay Tunnels
Courtesy of Russ Taylor

HAVING RECENTLY VISITED the tunnels, located deep within the white cliffs of Dover, I was delighted to meet a brave *National Trust* volunteer, Pete Legg. The tour was riveting for many reasons, and I cannot recommend it enough.

Wearing safety helmets equipped with headlights, we proceeded to descend some 70 feet, via 125 steep steps, into a world of total darkness. These man-made tunnels housed 185 armed forces personnel during the constant shelling raids over Dover. Once a hive of activity, they now lie eerily empty.

I should mention, it is not for the claustrophobic. Neither is there any speedy exit out of the tunnels once you are down there. Pitch-black tunnels loomed ominously away from the ones on which we were led, stirring within me a gradual sense of unease. Fearing I might spy something I would rather not see, I found myself focusing straight ahead.

Having acquired the tunnels in 2012, the *National Trust* needed experienced underground researchers to explore them. Initially, the team leader, Pete Legg, and one other, were the first people to venture into the tunnels. Having been closed for over forty years, and still possibly booby-trapped (the *M.O.D.* having done so in other similar tunnels) they were stepping into the unknown in more ways than one. In due course, miners and volunteers followed, proceeding to make them safe.

It has never occurred to me, that graffiti is something of interest - but to our guide, it provided an insight into those who had served down there, in times gone by. The significance of the graffiti is what indeed, links us to our ghost story.

It was in 2013 that the team were to realise the volume of graffiti needing to be analysed. The layout of the tunnels having been established and all remedial work carried out, the tours began in July 2015. In the process of surveying the graffiti late one afternoon, Pete took a photograph of five names etched into the rock face. *(See photograph 1.)* It was in 2017, having checked (as is routine practice) no damage had been inflicted on graffiti and artefacts he had made reference to during his tour, he, as the last person down there, locked the tunnels, and headed home. First to arrive the next day, he dutifully ventured down once more. Glancing momentarily at the graffiti as he passed, he noticed something was different about the group of five signatures: five had now become four! The rock face was undamaged – unchanged, to all intents and purposes - save for the fact that the top signature was now missing.

Pete showed us the original photograph, consisting of five names. Witnessing the graffiti ourselves, we could see there were now only four signatures. There is no evidence of defacement on the rock face. What has become of Jock Watson? *(see photograph 2)*. The question remains unanswered.

Both graffiti images courtesy of Pete Legg

Pete went on to tell two more mysterious tales: on another occasion a fellow-guide chided co-workers for playing tricks on him. Chains are hung down in the tunnels, restricting access into certain areas. The guide asked colleagues to stop tormenting him by swinging these chains. All were adamant they had done no such thing. However, one incident was to instigate a future visit by a Paranormal Investigation Team.

One tour group consisted of one woman and several men. Groups are normally limited to a number of no more than twelve. This one totalled fourteen, creating a situation where, in the confines of a tunnel, the party became spread wide. The guide at one point was concerned that the only lady in the party, located at the end of a long line, had not heard what he had said.

'It was quite okay,' she assured him. *'The lady stood next to me relayed what you said.'* 'The lady' had even identified herself as Edith to our lone female tourist in the group!

Two things are of significance at this point. Whilst walking this complex labyrinth of tunnels, a continual headcount is both compulsory and necessary. The tunnels go off at tangents for several miles. Anyone getting lost in them would most definitely never find their way out again. At no time had the headcount number changed. Secondly, an Edith Burvil is listed as having been a *N.A.A.F.I.* cook, working in these very tunnels. Edith was killed in a shelling raid on 10th February 1943, aged 39. Were they one and the same person? Curiosity, rather than fear, getting the better of all concerned, the help of a local Paranormal Investigation Team was called upon.

Pete was present come the night of the investigations. *EMF* meters (Electromagnetic flow meters), digital temperature fluctuation equipment, and all else needed to seek out a ghost, was transported down into this dark subterranean world. Come 2 a.m. they gave up

- any phantoms that night having no inclination *'to come to the party'*. However, heading via the tunnels to the lighthouse for a much-needed cup of tea, as soon as they entered it, all the equipment went into overdrive. There was indeed a riot of activity! So, there we have it, a vanishing signature, chains swung by an unseen hand, and a phantom tour guide named Edith. Having heard the tale of Edith, I was always a little concerned from then on, that she might choose to tap me on the shoulder, and make herself known to me. Should you choose to go, you may well meet her!

I cannot thank Pete enough, for permission to use the photographs, and for all his help. *Fan Bay Tours* operate daily; check in advance as to opening times - they do vary.

Interior of Lighthouse at Fan Bay Deep Tunnels
Courtesy of Russ Taylor

3

SHRIEKS THROUGHOUT SHREWSBURY

WHAT BETTER PLACE to head next, but my home county, Shropshire, with more than its fair share of ghosts, ghouls, spirits - call them what you will! I could write a book on it alone, never leaving this county, such is its abundance of ghosts.

Making our way via train we reached Shrewsbury, Shropshire's county town, littered with medieval buildings, some seeming to defy gravity by the level at which they lean. Add into the mix, its Abbey, the annual flower show - the town is well worth a visit. Dusk is shortly to be replaced by dark as we arrive by train at the county town, renowned for its many haunted abodes, and unexplained occurrences. Whichever way you arrive by train in Shrewsbury, the first landmarks are the Castle and the Abbey. Before leaving the station, glance across at Platform 3. You might well spot a lonely gent dressed in dark Victorian clothes. He stands patiently waiting for his train. His name was Thomas Thomas, MP for the town. The platform was redundant and inaccessible for many years, but has now been re-opened. Under the weight of heavy snowfall during the winter of 1888, the station roof collapsed on him, killing him outright as he waited for his London-bound train. Initially, many a fellow-passenger has called out to him, imagining he was unaware the platform was closed - only then to see him disappear before their eyes. Passengers may now encounter him stood beside them, as they await the arrival of their train.

Looking beyond the station you will see the Castle. Prior to the Castle being erected, properties of various sorts have stood on this land - one being a house. Its owner, a Mr Jack Blundell, was a wealthy man - both a brewer, and a draper - a well-established man of the town. He was also the town's infamous mass-murderer, six times wedded; five times widowed. With five of his wives vanishing without explanation, folk were starting to think this more than a little suspicious. I'm not sure whether I think the sixth wife noble or mad for even contemplating marrying such a man - her sister having been wife number five. When the opportunity arose, she set about her investigations. What she discovered was horrific…five complete sets of dismembered fingers hidden away in drawers. No accompanying bodies were ever found. He was hung on the outskirts of the town, but his spirit remains in the Castle grounds. He is seen leaving a ground floor door of the Castle, then to cross the lawn before vanishing. The building today is a military museum. Whilst here, you should pay it a visit.

Having now alighted from the train, glancing then to the right of the station, you will see *Shrewsbury Prison*. Though its solid wooden doors are now closed to prisoners, they are very much open to the likes of you and me, offering all manner of tours. It is a Victorian prison, built upon the site of a former Georgian one. The tours have excellent reviews on *TripAdvisor*.

Its dark, damp corridors lead to dismal cells. Descending deeper you will step into the claustrophobic tunnels, which can be viewed independently, or with a tour guide, often a former prison warden. It too can be viewed by way of a ghost tour at night. The bravest of the brave can even spend a night locked in a cell! Should I ever be afforded the opportunity to do so, I think I shall find my diary is already full. Check out *Jailhouse Tours* on the Internet for more details. There have been 73 executions, and several suicides carried out within the prison. Is it any wonder the place is haunted? It has housed many a murderer – one of those being Frank Griffin. Frank haunts the Tontine Hotel, Ironbridge (see chapter 29).

Inside Shrewsbury Prison
Josephinebeasley - Own work, CC BY-SA 4.0, https://commons.
wikimedia.org/w/index.php?curid=94293069

So, as you can see, we haven't even left the station platform yet, and already we have encountered three areas of interest, with some mesmerising tales related to them. Wending our way through the medieval cobbled streets and 'shuts', or alleyways, of Shrewsbury, we'll head to our first port-of-call, where I can guarantee you'll not be short on company of the ghost variety. Reputedly the most haunted building in the county town, welcome to the *Prince Rupert Hotel*!

During the evening you too can take a tour around our old and lovely town, with its black-and-white, timbered buildings - on a ghost tour no less! See the Tourist Information Office located in the Market Square for more details. I have done three - they are brilliant!

Shrewsbury was transformed into a major film set in 1984 when filming commenced for an adaptation of *'A Christmas Carol'* by Charles Dickens, and never was a place better chosen for the task! The stars and film crew all stayed at the *Prince Rupert*, George C Scott, Edward Woodward and Susannah York amongst them.

Ironically, the director of photography met with the hotel's 'Scrooge-like' character; the phantom was dressed in night cap and gown as he walked the corridor. The director even bade him goodnight. It was only when our Dickensian spirit walked through the wall that the director realised all was not as it should be. *'Fair shook up!'* by the experience, he fled to the bar at speed. The cast and crew from then on chose to head to their rooms in numbers of two or more.

The Town Crier, Martin Wood, standing 7 foot 2 inches in height, the world's tallest town crier, played the double role as the ghost of 'Christmas Future' and 'Christmas Present' in the film. He also doubled as Hagrid in the *Harry Potter* films. Head to the Market Square, to the Information Centre, or look his name up on the Internet to learn more about him. The *Prince Rupert Hotel* is to be found in Butchers' Row. If you should choose to stay – enjoy!

Ghost-touring groups pay visits to a recently-discovered cellar in the *Prince Rupert Hotel*, where a very unfriendly spirit is said to reside, by all accounts. With the intention of constructing a gym in the basement of the hotel, builders lifted floorboards, only to find a stone spiral staircase. This led to an old kitchen, where within, awaiting their arrival, was none other than a skeleton. Having made this discovery, another then followed - that of a doorway leading into a second room in the cellar. The ghost frequenting this room is someone folk might nowadays describe as 'having Anger Issues' - to say the least. He doesn't like being disturbed.

The manager generously allowed me to take photographs of the hotel. The receptionist, taking me on a tour, offered to take me down into the cellars to take photographs. I declined - with gusto!

The receptionist said he often felt as if he were being watched, especially when on a night shift. He did his level best to push tales to the back of his mind. The cleaner agreed wholeheartedly with him - ignorance is bliss!

We have, in this Grade 2 listed medieval building, no less than six active ghosts. The hotel comprises 70 en suite rooms, some located in the 12th century *Mansion House* wing; others are to be found in the later 15th century wing. Besides our unhappy soul in the cellar, you too may meet with our aforementioned 'Wee Willie Winkie' on his nightly patrol down the dim corridors - or Martha, who flits from the cellars, then up to the stairs. Hovering in hallways and doorways, her presence experienced everywhere!

Still there are others: two jilted wed-to-be lovers, whose spirits inhabit both rooms 7 and 5, who, according to the Visitors' Book, are still very much 'alive'. Then, last but not least, a young little fella. Standing alone on the perimeter wall, he answers to 'Thomas' when the mediums call. You'll be pleased to know such was the disruptive activity by the jilted bride to be in room 5 it has now been converted into a Conference Room! The town crier, Martin Wood, in his book *'Haunted Shrewsbury'* – which, I add, is an excellent read – tells the tale of one occurrence with this somewhat crotchety ghost. No one was standing anywhere near the lady in question at the time the incident took place in the cellars - so, anyone playing a prank can be ruled out.

I narrate the experience as if I were this unfortunate lady, bless her soul:

'Why did I even choose to go to this cellar, not long since discovered, located in this hotel's basement below, where there had been found a skeleton recently uncovered? It had lain there for god knows how long. To disturb it seemed insensitive, dangerous - possibly, somehow, wrong?

So, what on earth possessed me then - to take a photograph! And how I screamed when next this ghost, through me, displayed his wrath, grasping the clasp of my necklace, and pulling it taut. Before you venture, take my advice - give it further thought'.

Shrewsbury Castle

The Lion Hotel

Dim corridor of The Prince Rupert Hotel
All courtesy of Russ Taylor

4

THE NAG'S HEAD

WE HEAD OFF next in the direction of a Grade 1 listed building, to a splendid former coaching inn - the *Lion Hotel*. Its past visitors include, amongst others, Charles Dickens, Benjamin Disraeli, violinist Paganini, who performed in the hotel in 1833, and finally, none other than Madame Tussaud. The *Lion*, too, plays host to a variety of phantom friends, but more about them later. The public house opposite - The *Nag's Head* - is a building that you may wish to know more about.

From the outside it appears shabby, and quite ordinary. Inside, it is far from ordinary! You will find located on its upper floor, one particularly strange room. It is rarely visited by anyone - including its landlord. For many years, due to a number of suicides having been committed within the building, the Town Council deemed it unsuitable for hire. Within this extraordinary room there is a cupboard. Situated on the inside of this cupboard door is to be found a painting (see later photograph). It is reported by those who have seen it, as being crude in style, and described as having a sinister look about it, which is hardly surprising, given its history. It depicts a naked, bearded man. It is said that no matter how often it has been painted over, the painting reappears. Well - you decide if you believe that or not.

I'm not sure whether I think Philip incredibly brave, or undoubtedly bonkers (possibly both), merely for having the temerity to visit the room, let alone to photograph the painting - but fair play to him! When I emailed him to ask permission to use his photograph of the painting, he said of the experience

'I can happily say that, so far at least, there haven't been any ill effects (at least none that I'm aware of!) from seeing the picture. It is a genuinely eerie thing though, really unsettling, I don't blame you for wanting to avoid it!'

This room, it would seem, is inexplicably influenced by this painting. Three content, happy people, during a night spent within it, have been driven to commit suicide. One former guest had thrown herself out of its window during the night's stay. Others having visited the room have met with a variety of accidents shortly afterwards. It would appear to be infested by ill-fate. It is included in every ghost tour, but 'the forbidden room' is only ever viewed from the pavement below. Frankly, each time I pass the *Nag's Head* I scurry by. I certainly have no desire to look up at its window. You, on the other hand, might relish the thought of doing so. More information can be found on the website *www.hauntedpubs.com*. Who, or whatever is in the building, also likes to play tricks. The juke-box has been known, on more than the odd occasion, to play in the dead of night - despite being unplugged!

If I had to compare this room with one other, I would liken it to that residence well-known to the ghost-hunting fraternity, 50 Berkeley Square, Mayfair, London. Both buildings, as will be revealed, have seen too many fatalities for comfort. The descriptions of events are mirror images of those occurring in our Shrewsbury public house....but we'll return to Berkeley Square in a short while.

The Nag's Head – the cursed painting Courtesy of Philip Davies Celebrant

With countless tales still to be told, sadly it is time - for now at least – to bid farewell to Shrewsbury, as we head south to the historic town of Ludlow, where is to be found a hotel in which there are spirits galore! Its fame guarantees that it is visited by tourist parties simply devoted to the task of seeking 'them' out. Brave folk they are indeed!

5

LOST SOULS IN LUDLOW

THE FEATHERS HOTEL

If you are a woman, do not stay in room 211! Female guests have experienced having their hair pulled, being pinched, and one, even dragged from her bed. Some have woken with inexplicable bruises come morning. Gents, on the other hand, have been known to be 'fondly caressed'. Venturing further down towards room 232-233, you might meet with a gent dressed in Victorian clothes, accompanied by his dog. All appears fine and dandy until both walk through the wall. If that were not enough, children are heard tapping and clapping as they run through the corridors in the middle of the night. Unruly children are bad enough - that they be from 'the other side', heaven help us! *HH & Spooky nights* hold regular ghost hunts here, check the internet for one of many on offer.

THE BLUE BOAR INN

Even if you feel in need of a stiff drink to get over the escapades in the *Feathers*, you may wish to avoid the *Blue Boar Inn*. If, on the other hand, you can't get enough of our ghostly friends, this is the place for you, given it has no less than five! Each floor has a resident ghost. They include a pipe-smoking gent, dressed in a 1930s suit, a bonneted old lady in Victorian-style dress - a fifteen- year-old girl, a Cavalier soldier, and a dapper chap in a blue tunic, with silver gilt buttons. You could almost believe you had crashed a fancy-dress party by mistake.

Whilst having a drink in the bar, keep an eye on the time. During times of paranormal activity, the clock is known to suddenly speed up. The front door, too, opens of its own accord, not pushed open, but pulled! Most importantly, watch your drinks – they are often tipped over by an unseen hand.

I often wondered if ghostly occupants sharing a property, such is as the case at the Blue Boar, are aware of each other? Whether, in fact, they might even interact with one another? Having watched episodes of *Most Haunted,* I am informed that spirits undoubtedly are aware of one another! Some taking sanctuary from the more sinister apparitions they share the property with.

THE GLOBE INN

A Tudor soldier, Edward Dobson, haunts the *Globe Inn*. Murdered within the property in a brawl in 1553, he appears bewigged and cloaked, thus being easily recognisable. Up until the time of his death, he was stationed at Ludlow Castle under Richard Duke of York. The Castle also is said to be haunted by Marion La Bruyere. An illicit affair culminated in Marion slitting her secret lover's throat. So distraught was she, she then threw herself from the tower. Come dusk you may well see her. On the anniversary of her suicide - you may even hear her screams.

THE BULL HOTEL

Should you choose to stay in the *Bull Hotel,* you may make the acquaintance of a priest, who by his looks appears to be somewhat disgruntled, or that of a ghostly little girl, Gertrude, or 'Gertie' (as she likes to be called), who was crushed by a raging bull in the nearby slaughter yard. Following the discovery of a previously unknown priest hole in the hotel, visitors and staff began to hear the tread of footsteps in uninhabited rooms. Visitors to the *Bull Hotel* also feel they have been tapped on the shoulder, only to turn and find no one is there. Others lay claim to also having witnessed glasses move of their own accord behind the bar.

As ever, I could go on, but the best way as always, should you wish to learn more, is to join a ghost tour. Visit the tourist office for more details, or book a room of course (*see the www.ghostpubs.com* website).

Ludlow is an idyllic medieval market town, with many individual shops and superb restaurants. It is some 20 miles south of Shrewsbury. However - having many places yet to visit, we must wave a fond farewell to Ludlow.

6

SIN-EATERS - RATLINGHOPE

Tombstone of the last 'Sin-eater'
Courtesy of Russ Taylor

HEADING NORTH TO Church Stretton, travelling by either rail or road, you may wish to ascend to the beautiful heath and moorland area, the much admired Long Mynd. It is noted as an 'Area of Outstanding Natural Beauty'. It is home also to the Stiperstones, and The Devil's Chair, an unusual rock formation, with legendary stories related to it. It is mightily impressive and very high - awash in purple by late summer, thanks to a carpet of heather. The journey up to it is by way of a narrow road, which is not one for the faint-hearted. With no barriers to prevent you hurtling over the edge, you could find yourself hundreds of feet below in Carding Mill Valley.

But trust me, taking time out to make a detour to Ratlinghope (pronounced 'Ratchup' by the locals) as we head north west, is well-justified. This tiny village, four miles west of Church Stretton, and twelve miles south of Shrewsbury, is infamous for a most unlikely and bizarre reason. In St. Margaret's churchyard is the grave of Richard Munslow, recognised as the last known person in Britain to have been a 'Sin-eater'. Sin-eaters were ordinarily paupers, the lowliest of the low. In repayment for food, drink and money, they would stand at the graveside of the dead. In a ritual that consisted of devouring bread, beer or wine, they would take on the sins of the corpse being buried, enabling the soul to be permitted to enter heaven - and so to find peace in death. Strangely, Mr Munslow, who was buried in 1906, was neither a pauper nor a beggar, but in fact an established farmer in the area. The ritual was prevalent in the Marches on the English/Welsh border, and also practised in North Wales. There is little evidence that it occurred elsewhere.

'Sin-eaters' were community outcasts. Locals believed them to be infested by the evil deeds they had consumed during the ritual. They lived as recluses until needed, and were treated much like lepers. The church frowned upon the practice, but chose to turn a blind eye to it.

Ratlinghope also hosts the most extraordinary funeral procession, it being a Victorian phantom one no less! To the dubious - the sceptical, I should add - a visiting vicar from far off Brighton was one such person to have witnessed this dramatic scene. Whilst out walking, the funeral parade appeared before him. On return to his friend's home, in a jovial manner, he described what he had seen.

Munslow's Tombstone – St. Margaret's church.
Campaigners' raised £1000 to restore the grave.
Courtesy of Russ Taylor

He enquired of his friend as to who it was that might have chosen such an eccentric funeral. Imagine his face when his friend told him. By the way, the vicar never returned to Ratlinghope. All in all, it is worth a visit, and quaint it is too!

THE PHANTOM FUNERAL OF RATLINGHOPE

And from out of nowhere appeared the procession.
Two black horses adorned in ostrich plumes and velvet drapes,
steered by the hearse-master, suitably sombre for the occasion,
in top hat, tailcoat, and carriage cape.
Behind him, the carriage hearse, then the remainder of the funeral
pageant,
each dressed in their best black, bustle dresses, gloves, bonnets, and a
shawl...
then alongside the coffin, the pall-bearers,
all walking at a uniform pace...
when suddenly they vanished, in but a matter of seconds,
as they crossed the bridge without a trace.
No sooner had they appeared, then they were gone!
on this dusty country lane, where, only a moment ago,
had there been neither sight nor sound of anyone...
Save for me and my faithful dog-
who, for the time being, had gone to ground.
He for now, one cowering, quivering, petrified hound.
The distinctive sound of the trot of horses' hooves prevailed -
there was no other noise. No one spoke, no one wept,
not a single soul wailed, at the phantom funeral parade.

7

LONDON
A WORD IF I MAY...

'CURIOSITY KILLED THE cat' - a warning of the dangers that lie in wait for those inclined to pursue things that are best left to rest in peace.

I'd like to say the term 'killed' maybe an exaggeration of what might become of those with a lurid fascination (in this case in the spirit world) but in two tales I shall relate, there are certain properties - one in London, where, for whatever reason, deaths occurred. These might have been triggered by hysteria, but there was a fatal outcome on more than the odd occasion. Fortunately for us, I have not heard of any guests dying in any hotels and hostelries in recent times. That is not to say you are guaranteed a stress free stay, I hasten to add!

Many parks, squares, streets, stations, buildings, hotels included of course, were constructed upon leper and plague burial sites.

The city has witnessed many murders and public executions. There have been unfortunate natural disasters, and in recent times, terrorist attacks. It comes as no surprise therefore, to learn that all manner of places are frequented by more than the odd roaming ghost.

London is steeped in history and blessed with the most beautiful and magnificent buildings, palaces, museums and restaurants. It also possesses something that strikes colossal fear into most men, manifesting itself in the form of shops, lots of them - some very expensive.

For the majority, a trip to the capital from the provinces is often made by train. One then proceeds to take a cab to a carefully chosen hotel... but which one?

8

SOMEWHERE TO STAY

The Langham Hotel

For those whose enthusiasm knows no end in their quest to meet with those 'on the other side', a stay at *'The Langham'* is a must. A variety of 'non-paying guests' reside here - seven in fact. If you are feeling exceptionally brave (many might say mad) Room 333 is the one for you. If on the other hand, you are of the opposite inclination, it's best to look elsewhere.

ROOM 333
In 1973 James Alexander Gordon, radio announcer for the BBC, awoke to see a ball of light hovering before him, changing into a form of a man clothed in Victorian evening dress.

One always tends to say what one may, or may not do in any given situation. We have a tendency to do the exact opposite of what, initially, we supposed we might, but I can genuinely say I would not have taken Mr Gordon's course of action - that being to speak to the apparition - especially, since the spectre in question seemed more than a little disgruntled to be asked who 'he' was. With that it headed towards him in the most ferocious fashion - at speed! Mr Gordon fled from his bed at much the same pace, begging the next question - would you have returned to the room? Would curiosity have got the better of you? Do you know, crazy as it sounds, I don't honestly know what I would have done. Mr Gordon did just that, choosing to confront his spectre - with a colleague in tow of course! His ghostly room-mate, still in-situ, seemed less ominous than before, and eventually faded away.

Mr Gordon is by no means the only person to have experienced what he did. Many a person has related the same tale, unaware, it should be emphasised, that previous guests had encountered the same situation, as is often the case in many a haunted abode.

Should you find yourself allocated a room in one of The Langham's upper floors, you might happen upon a tall silver haired gent adorned in a flowing cloak and cravat. Witnesses have initially viewed him as harmless - merely someone who likes to dress eccentrically. Residents and staff - I hasten to tell you - would say otherwise. They describe an encounter with him as a truly terrifying experience. Transfixing all he meets with a deathly zombie-like stare, he stalks the silent, dimly lit hallways. But who is he? I shudder as I type, merely at the thought of those blank staring eyes.

Many consider the 'dapper chap' who frequents the upper floors to be the ghost of 'Doctor Death'. It is said that on their honeymoon night, the newly-wed doctor murdered his bride; he then committed suicide.

On the other hand, should you be designated room 632, you might well find yourself on the floor in the middle of the night. It is said many an unfortunate guest has been shoved from his or her bed by some unseen force.

For an interim period, the BBC occupied the building. Night staff often had their sleep disrupted in much the same way, in this same room.

In July 2014, the England cricket team, reserved rooms at *The Langham Hotel*. Stuart Broad was one of several for whom nights were somewhat stressful. Broad, too hot to sleep, suddenly felt he was not entirely alone in the room. Coinciding with this there followed the sound of the bathroom taps being turned on. Switching the room light on to see what was going on, the taps turned themselves off. On switching his room light off, once again the taps switched themselves back on.

Other team-mates experienced strange things afoot. Wives and girlfriends chose to leave. Of Broad - he vacated the room, moving in to share with Prior whose room was twin bedded. The episode made headline news in the Daily Mail newspaper.

A phantom butler has been seen wandering the corridors, only then to simply vanish in mid-air. Others have seen a young woman in the same vicinity as the butler.

In another room you may well make the acquaintance of a liveried footman, complete with powdered wig. Thankfully he is a harmless soul.

The only strange thing (other than seeing a man from the eighteenth century in your room of course) is the sudden and inexplicable sharp drop in temperature.

The ghost most often seen is a German prince, wearing a military jacket; he is described as stocky in build. He committed suicide in the hotel, jumping from the fourth floor.

The crème de la crème have all stayed here: Princess Diana; Wallis Simpson; Noel Coward, to name but a few.

Sir Arthur Conan Doyle stayed and chose the hotel as the setting for one of his stories 'The Sign of Four'. One other notable visitor is Napoleon the Third. He liked it so much, he still resides here. You may well happen upon him, should you be wandering the lower corridors at night. Not the most handsome of folk - he has a horrid gash on his face and is truly petrifying, apparently.

To all those alighting at Portland Place, sleep well.

THE GEORGIAN HOUSE HOTEL

Described as an elegant and stylish 4 Star boutique hotel with excellent reviews and inhabited by children, albeit of the spirit form.

A feeling of dread falls upon me each time I discover there are children anywhere within the vicinity of my hotel room. In fact, if truth be told, give me an adult only hotel any day. Given that these children are not of the mortal kind - no thank you! There is something decidedly chilling, to my mind at least, when I am told a building is haunted by children.

Guests have complained about the noise levels of children playing upstairs and in corridors, only then to be told there are no children currently residing in the hotel.

We shall, in due course visit other hotels throughout England with phantom occupants, some establishments making good incomes by advertising the fact – and why not! Personally, I am very glad they do.

GRANGE BLOOMS HOTEL

With a trip to London in the offing, I thought it only fair to throw caution to the wind, and stay at one of the listed haunted hotels - thus opting for the Grange Blooms. Well - what can I say, but that I experienced a novel sensation, one I have never felt before, and have no desire to repeat! It occurred whilst talking to a receptionist, who was relating an experience that had happened to him, during his first week of employment there.

He had no idea at the time, that the hotel was haunted. The incident occurred whilst he was happily studying a painting. A table lamp situated to his right, with an extremely stiff on/off switch, was suddenly switched on.

He demonstrated to me how difficult it is to push the switch from right to left and vice versa. The disturbing thing for us both, as he described what had happened, was that we both felt suddenly and inexplicably chilled. So disconcerting was it - we both felt the need to leave the room. Moving only a few feet, both our body temperatures returned to normal. Now, some may say, and I wouldn't disagree, it may have been our imaginations running riot. Quite why both of us shuddered at exactly the same time, intrigues me. The best way I can describe the sensation is likewise, when one declares *someone has just walked over my grave*. The sensation ordinarily lasts for a few seconds. We all recognise the cold tingle that makes us shudder involuntarily. However - this lasted longer. Whilst we remained in the room, the feeling of goose bumps, never left either of us.

He went on to tell me that, one night, the security team had seen, on camera, the figure of a man walk across the room downstairs. The figure walked into the kitchen. Staff headed down to apprehend what they assumed to be an intruder, only to find there was no one in the kitchen, or anywhere else in any of the rooms on this floor. All the doors and windows were securely locked from the inside; thus no one could have escaped via this route.

In the dead of night, the night porter regularly witnesses the hotel lift being summoned up to the third floor. Having arrived there, it then descends back to the ground floor – upon which, its doors open, but with no one visibly within it. I should add, this never occurs during the hours of daylight.

If you should be allocated room 103, accept it at your peril. It has been the scene of much activity. One guest fled terrified from the shower. Fleeing to Reception, still dripping wet, her modesty was saved only by a towel wrapped around her. Comfort was duly administered, and a new room allocated to the distressed guest.

There have been two suicides in the hotel - one at least - I was informed - in room 103.

The murder of a child (who, incidentally, is heard weeping in the kitchen area late at night) is also reported. The parents believed their child to be possessed by the devil, and so in turn murdered their own offspring. How awful is that!

It is also believed by staff that a former hotel owner also haunts the building.

One of its other former occupants, the Reverend John Cumming, still frequents the property today. Wishing no offence to the Reverend, I think it fair to say he would not head many a list of dinner party invitees. The life and soul of any happy party he was not! Minister to the National Scottish Church, situated in Covent Garden during the 1800s- he was very much opposed to the Catholic faith, preaching with a passion against all who followed it.

One of his favourite past times when 'off duty', he liked nothing more than to scour the Old and New Testaments. It is well recorded he was a person with an insatiable appetite for all to do with the prediction of the end of the world. Is he still scouring the Testaments in the hotel library as I type?

In summing it up, there was an air of unease throughout the hotel. Whether that was because I had prior knowledge of the hotel's history... well possibly. However, I note, having read other guest reviews, they too mention how eerie it felt.

The Langham Hotel
Illustration of The Langham accessible via Wikipedia

It saddens me to say, it is now in need of some tender loving care. Tired décor leaves one disenchanted. Perhaps this will be soon remedied.

If, on the other hand, you are looking for an active ghost experience - well an American family have just spent 10 days there, prior to my arrival. They came armed with all the latest technology, in an attempt to seek out whoever lingers there. I wasn't able to speak to them. Frankly I am rather glad I wasn't!

There will of course, be many other hotels in London with non-paying phantom guests!

The 'Cold Room'
Courtesy of Russ Taylor

9

HAUNTING THE BOARDS

WELL, HAVING READ much on those who tread the boards one way or another in London's theatres, I have concluded it would be far easier to list those theatres not haunted! If you are seeking an in-depth book into the subject of London's theatres, you can do no better than Gilly Pickup's *Haunted West End*. It is superbly written, and a feast of facts and stories.

The number of murders that have happened in various theatres is quite staggering - one over a costume wig no less. Now that really is a 'bad hair day' for you! One victim's body remained undiscovered until renovation work commenced many years later. Suicides, too, seem to have been quite commonplace. No wonder there are spirits galore frequenting the theatres.

I think we shall alight first at the *Theatre Royal* in Drury Lane, where it would seem there is never a dull moment. This building plays host to four ghosts (two murdered in the theatre itself) one of a decapitated clown, who likes to join the audience in his appreciation of the show. If you have a fear of clowns (Coulrophobia) and a fear of ghosts (Phasmophobia) heaven help you!

The other poor soul murdered in this theatre is a gentleman who appears dressed in grey. He has been seen regularly by staff and actors over a long period of time. He is believed to be the gentleman whose skeleton was found by builders. He always leaves via the wall, where his skeleton was discovered. If allocated the end seat of the fourth row in the upper circle, you will have shared his seat. Apparently, he watches rehearsals from here, so he won't ask you to vacate the seat, should you be allocated it.

You may recall my mention of the 'tiff over the wig'. Thankfully this spirit remains backstage.

We come to the third spirit, that of a bodiless clown, thought to be Joseph Grimaldi. Grimaldi had a bizarre fear of death (Necrophobia). Did he fear being buried alive – who knows? He requested he be decapitated after his death - thus ensuring he was 'dead'.

Perhaps not a bad idea as I digress to tell you the story of a poor guest back at *The Lion Hotel* in Shrewsbury. During the 1800s one guest was taken ill. Later that same night, events took a turn for the worse, when he was pronounced dead. Fearing 'bad press', and it being before the days of refrigeration, he was duly buried in the night in the graveyard just across the road from the hotel. Before long, noises were heard coming from the graveyard. Naturally, on hearing such a thing, most people's inclination was to head in the opposite direction, but eventually the curate, a more courageous person than I, located the noise as coming from this gent's newly-dug grave. The coffin was exhumed. The inside of the coffin lid was covered in scratch-marks. The flesh on his fingers was badly torn. Needless to say, he had died of suffocation, and so was then reburied. His wails are still heard on many a gloomy night.

Referring back to Joseph Grimaldi, his grave can be found in Islington in the park named after him. Should you find yourselves in the City on the first Sunday in February, there is an annual Clowns service. The service has recently been relocated to the *All Saints Church* on Livermere Road. It is a service like no other, in that there is much 'clowning around in the pews'. The service commemorates Grimaldi and all fellow clowns having passed to the 'other side', so to speak. The *Holy Trinity* is recognised as the Clowns' Church. The service is extremely popular, so get there early to view the congregation of clowns, heading to church in their best red noses, the weirdest and whackiest of wigs, and most splendiferous of costumes.

Only a stone's throw away from here is the *Clowns' Gallery* and Museum located in Cumberland Close. The safety of the building hangs in the balance as at July 2019. Check in advance to see if it is still open. I do hope so. Even I, no clown-lover, found it to be a fascinating place to visit. On entering, fairground music could be heard playing in the background. It was a delightful visit. The stained-glass window of Grimaldi is also worth seeing.

Whilst in the area I suggest you go to the *Museum of Curiosities* as well – but only if you are not easily disturbed, apparently. I am told it is not for the faint-hearted. How to describe it to you? Well, not giving too much away, it is a small chamber of all that is bizarre, berserk and horrendously gruesome on occasions. See *YouTube* or *TripAdvisor* to learn more about it. Bethnal Green tube station is the nearest stop to alight at.

Finally, returning to the subject of theatres and that of the spirit of Grimaldi! He often tends to appear behind people seated in the boxes.

HE'S BEHIND YOU!

Poor unsuspecting folk, quite unaware,
that suspended it seemed by nothing,
had appeared behind them in mid-air,
the face of a disembodied circus clown!
Smiling benignly whilst looking down,
it turned first to glance upon the cast.
All who saw him were speechless - aghast.
And then it turned as if to acknowledge us -
the audience sat here below.

He had a white chalked face,
strangely protruding, bulbous eyes,
painted, ruddy red lips and cheeks –
but we'd no desire to see clowns or freaks!
His grotesque face - so animated -
now was all aglow.
Grabbing hats and coats,
unanimously it was decided
it was time to go!

Her Majesty's Theatre Phantom of the Opera
Attributed to Seth Anderson Wikipedia commons

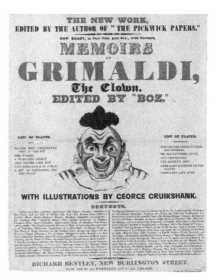

The Fortune Theatre
The Woman in Black
Accessible Wikipedia commons

Grimaldi
Illustration accessible via Wikipedia Public Domain

The Royal Albert Hall
Courtesy of Russ Taylor

The final ghost at Drury Lane is one you are unlikely to encounter, but many a famous performer has. The spirit in question - Dan Leno - was a Victorian comedian and actor. He was mostly remembered as a pantomime dame, and for his clog dances. Sadly, alcoholism haunted him. He also suffered with severe mental problems. Hopefully his days in the theatre are happier now, the inner demons plaguing him now laid to rest.

We'll take a short stroll across to the *Fortune Theatre*, home to the spine-chilling play '*The Woman in Black*'. As if the plot were not scary enough in itself – yes, you guessed correctly, the theatre is haunted by - a woman in black. I joke not! She is seen in a lower box, and occasionally hovers in the bar.

Heading to Shaftsbury Avenue we come upon the *Palace Theatre*, where two seats are permanently reserved for its residing spirits. If only I knew which two seats they were, for I would not want to be sat either side of them! We have visited the *Palace Theatre* twice in the last year. I didn't know anything of our spirit residents, but I wasn't surprised to learn it had two ghosts - it is by far the most eerie of the theatres. I would not like to visit it when it is empty.

Continuing down Shaftsbury Avenue, then heading onto Haymarket, we arrive eventually at *Her Majesty's Theatre*, home to '*The Phantom of the Opera*'. It is actually haunted by 'a phantom', who resides in the upper box, on the right-hand side of the theatre. He has also been seen hovering at the back of the stalls. Request seats either in the circle or in the front stalls, and all should prove stress free - unless your desire is to make the acquaintance of the phantom, of course.

A useful tip – purchase seats too high up in the theatre and you won't see the whole show, and all its special effects. My husband and I have visited the theatre six times to watch the musical, once from the Royal Box. It has a dreadful view. You can only see a third of the stage. '*The Phantom of the Opera*' is superb. If you have never seen it – please do! Best description of it is a pitcher full of thrillingly chilling content with an abundance of romance thrown in for good measure.

Some may recall Tommy Cooper collapsing on stage at Her Majesty's Theatre, and dying shortly after. It is rumoured he puts in the odd appearance even to this day.

There are plenty of other ghosts, lingering at their leisure, in all manner of theatres all over London, and throughout the rest of Great Britain too.

The more energetic amongst us can head from here on foot, but if you're feeling a little weary, take a cab, tube or bus to Kensington for our next destination, the *Royal Albert Hall*.

Ghostly goings-on became such a problem here, it made headline news in the *Independent* in 1996. It is a rather '*Phantom of the Opera*'- like story. The *Hall's* organ constructor - Father Willis - wearing a black skullcap, was paying too frequent a visit for comfort - for some at least. Two more ghosts wander the building, these being the ghosts of two Victorian ladies. Prior to the construction of the *Hall*, there once stood a house on the site. Its occupant was the Count d'Orsay. Cutting a long story short – it is worth mentioning that a brothel was run in the basement of the house, which begs the question - are these perhaps, former ladies of the night?

I think it fair to say, we think of actors as being talented – creative – emotional. Most of all (if one dare say it) they are in fact, very superstitious! Here follows some of the traditions still in operation today, ensuring the stage demons are mollified, for the performance at least:-

KEEPING THE DEMONS AT BAY

No blue, green, yellow to be worn. No peacock feathers displayed on the stage.

No real mirrors. No bouquets. No authentic jewels - only paste.

No good luck words to be uttered.

The ghost light as ever to be left on. No one must peep through the curtain.

Leave the dressing room - left foot first!

Each performer must be pinched.

The Mac**** word must not be heard. No one person (save for stagehands) must whistle.

No final bows must be rehearsed.

No final line of the play has been rehearsed, heretofore spoken.

And, God forbid, let there be no knitters in the wings!

Opening performances must never be programmed for a Friday night.

The theatre should be shut one day a week, so thespian spirits can rehearse their roles.

Best not upset them, for they can be such temperamental souls!

No rules of superstition have here to been broken.
No demons, thankfully, awoken.

Actors whose names I have come across who admit to having encountered various ghosts, include Dame Judi Dench, Patrick Stewart, Arthur Askey, Thora Hird and Sir Harry Secombe, Dame Margaret Rutherford, Roy Hudd, Jasper Carrot, Clive Carter, Donald Sinden, Les Dawson and Barbara Windsor. I'm sure there are many more. One must remember, for every person who has spoken of such an experience, several have not, for fear of appearing delusional.

There are a variety of backstage theatre tours, and fascinating in a variety of ways they are too. Check out the Internet to join one.

10

A COSTUME CURSED

THIS IS A true story of an event experienced by Dame Thora Hird. The bolero jacket was worn during performances of a 1940s' play '*THE QUEEN CAME BY*'.

I discovered the story in a book, '*Haunted West End*'. The book's author, Gilly Pickup, kindly granted me permission to adapt her account of events, into the form of a poem. I'm pleased to say she adored it!

The cause of such unrest and suspicion - superstition -
why even rumoured to be possessed!
A local priest, in times gone by, had been summoned,
in the hope bad influences might be suppressed.
Appeasing many a fearful actress, prayers were said -
even so, most still refused to wear it...

And so, there it remained in the costume store;
boxed and shelved, dust gathering on its lid,
covered with brown paper;
out of sight - well hid.

Relevant to this tale I must tell -
it was a Victorian jacket,
with a high-necked collar; important to recall,
throughout rehearsals, it had fitted her **well!**

At the first performance, standing centre of stage,
both collar and jacket, by some strange force,
began to constrict – inflicting such pressure

she could barely breathe - let alone sing!
It was as if this costume's guardian angel
was stood in the wings.

The seamstress was summoned the very next day –
'*Expand both collar and jacket without delay.*'
And so it was, and yet still it was tight,
and there in the wings, whatever the theatre,
remained this presence - this force every night.

All who tried the costume on felt somehow 'restrained'.
Nothing ventured, nothing gained,
to find an answer to the mystery -
to learn the history of this costume's owner -
as yet unknown, so far unheard of?
Mediums were employed,
communicating through thought and by word.

On the play's final night,
the costume itself took centre stage.
The whole situation was quite absurd.
A previous 'wearer' – Edith Merryweather,
an actress of the theatre -
on walking home with a lover had died - in a fall.
One must wonder, if indeed,
it was an accident at all?

*I wonder what became of the jacket?

11

50, BERKELEY SQUARE

THERE HAVE BEEN many stories relating to events connected to this property. In each article I happen upon, the story varies, but the gist of the events is much the same throughout - rather a case of Chinese whispers perhaps – who knows?

50, Berkeley Square has the reputation of being one of the most haunted houses in Britain. Amongst its many owners was the British Prime Minister, George Canning, who spoke of happenings both irrational and inexplicable occurring within the property. Nowadays it is an antiquarian book shop, *Maggs Bros. Ltd.* People still avoid the room in question. As was the case with *'The Nag's Head'* in Shropshire, many people, having been of sound and rational mind on entering the room, have gone on to take their own life during a night spent within it, or else been petrified witless by heaven only knows what! A Police notice was erected in the 1950s, forbidding anyone to enter the room in question. A rather infamous next-door neighbour to 50 Berkeley Square was Sir Winston Churchill, who lived at number 48 as a child. Robert Clive of India lived at number 45 for 13 years before committing suicide

Newspaper Cutting Berkeley Square
Courtesy of the Ghost Attic

there. I have strolled through Berkeley Square on many occasions. It is idyllic to the eye. I shall, in the future, see it in quite a different light.

I relate to you now, the fateful events that befell an innocent servant girl, working and living in 50, Berkeley Square. Her allocated sleeping quarters were in this abode's sinister attic. Screams were heard one night coming from the room. Those who came to her aid were unable to ascertain what it was that had struck such fear into the poor girl. Merely a nightmare perhaps? Yet by morning she was dead. Intrigued by the fate of the late servant, the master of the house, announced he would spend a night in the room. Having done so, a servant was quoted to have said, *'As God is my word, thirty minutes later, terrible screams were heard coming from the room, followed by the boom from a shot gun.'*

The master had been found dead on the floor; his face contorted in terror. Still the sceptical would not have it, and chose, individually, to follow in his footsteps, spending a night in the said room. One retiree to the room in question instructed, *'Should the bell be struck once, ignore it. If rung twice, aid will be needed. Come without delay!'*

All was fine until the clock struck midnight. The bell rang hard, fast and furious! The sight that met those who came to his aid was that of a man deranged. The coroner's records for the gent concerned read *'Death by Fright'*. Many London ghost tours include 50, Berkeley Square in them. You may want to see it for yourself.

As you can imagine, there are many walks to choose from – check the Internet as always.

One walk worth watching on *YouTube* is that of 'The Cursed Cobblestone', narrated by Richard Jones. Having seen it, I can guarantee you will never take anything that doesn't belong to you again!

12

A DEADLY SERIOUS BUSINESS!

The Premature Burial
https://en.wikipedia.org/wiki/File:Wiertz_burial.jpg

IN AN EFFORT to lure you out of London's inner city streets, and up to my next proposed port of call, I need to tell you a story – well, a few actually! A couple of these fascinating tales are somewhat macabre, but all true!

So, if you are sitting comfortably, then I'll begin.

By the 1800s London faced an awful dilemma. The population of the city grew fast and had actually doubled in the first half of the 19th Century. Consequently, the death rate also increased, to the point where the city was literally swamped with corpses. Often underground storage areas held the dead in stacks some twenty coffins high, filling every available space. The stench emanating from poorly buried bodies, besides being rank-smelling, was dangerously toxic.

With an urgent necessity to deal with decomposing corpses, the coffins of the long since (and often - not so long since) departed occupants, were exhumed. A variety of reasons, gave cause to the coffins being opened and thus, a multitude of skeletons and decaying corpses was left on open ground. Some unceremoniously thrown into sewers, and the River Thames, with the inevitable effect of contaminating the water supply. It is worth noting that Churches sold the discarded coffins for the purpose of firewood to the poorest in society. Now that's what you call a re-cycling initiative! But pause a moment, if you will, to consider what the smell of the wood being burnt was like!

Additionally, epidemics such as cholera, typhoid, measles and smallpox ran rife through the population. Like a stack of tumbling dominoes, each new problem instigated another, all contributing to the seemingly insoluble dilemma of what to do with London's dead!

Victims of cholera often fell into a coma. Given that bodies were buried swiftly in an effort to control the spread, many more people than was ideal were buried alive!

1818 saw the publication of Mary Shelley's Gothic novel *Frankenstein*. It was immensely popular. Along with too many folk being laid to rest

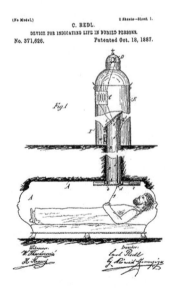
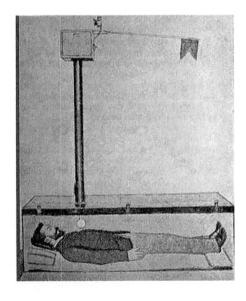

before they ought, and stories of corpses resurrected by electricity, a fear of being buried alive became commonplace amongst the Victorians. This fear is known as Taphophobia.

The publication of Edgar Allan Poe's short story *The Premature Burial* in 1844 added to the fear!

These stories engendered such trepidation in the general populace that some entrepreneurs of the day manufactured *Safety Coffins*. There were a few ingenious ways to ensure that life was extinct. Above ground a bell was erected over the grave. The bell rope was fed through the coffin, then wound around the hand of the corpse - *just in case*! The plan had one major shortcoming - they had not thought to put enough air vents in the coffin!

Grave-diggers were paid to listen out for the bell, hence the sayings- *saved by the bell* and *dead ringer*.

A further difficulty arose because no one had allowed for the fact that a rotting corpse would swell. As the body inflated, so in turn the bell was often activated! Can you imagine patrolling the cemetery at night and all those bells suddenly pealing!

No one is known to have been saved by this procedure.

Sometimes, glass was put in the coffin lid in front of the corpse's face to double check for signs of condensation. But perhaps the most alarmingly bizarre practice was *enema smoking* - we won't even go there - I'll leave it to your imagination.

It's worth mentioning that cremation was something regarded with much suspicion and believed to be indulged in only by those of a 'foreign persuasion'.

BODY SNATCHERS

Medical practices were advancing at a significant pace during the 18th and 19th centuries. As a consequence there was a shortage of bodies for medical students to dissect, so the macabre business of 'Body Snatching' developed. John Bishop and Thomas Williams were two of this new 'industry's' main protagonists, but by no means the only source. The hospitals of St. Bartholomew's, St. Thomas', and Kings College of Anatomy regularly paid for bodies to be supplied to them.

With the crime of body-snatching increasing, a regular nightly patrol of the graveyards became the norm. This caused a *production line* issue for Bishop and Williams; demand was outweighing supply; a new supply route was needed!

Aided by rum laced with laudanum, strangers were befriended, drugged and in due course murdered by the two men.

At this time, only the bodies of criminals were legally deemed acceptable for dissection. The irony of this tale is that, eventually, having been convicted of a multitude of murders, Bishop's and Williams' bodies were bequeathed to medical science!

ALL ABOARD!

Returning to the vexed question of suitable burial sites for London's dead, the proposal that the Government should fund seven 'Garden Cemeteries' was passed. These were to be established in the suburbs of London, one of the first was in Highgate (our next port of call). As a profit making business venture, the cemeteries were intended as resting places for the middle and upper classes...and popular they proved too! But what was to be done with the corpses of the lower classes?

In 1849 the London Necropolis Corporation was conceived. The idea was to ship the dead up the Thames to Waterloo Bridge Station from where they would be transported by train to the Brookwood Cemetery in Surrey. Both the dead and their mourners were accommodated in the appropriate 'class' for the journey. The sole purpose of this station being to transport the dead, it was named The London Necropolis Railway Station.

This cemetery is still the largest in the United Kingdom, and one of the biggest in Europe.

A NEW SIDE-LINE IN PHOTOGRAPHY

In researching all of this, I am astonished to discover that the Victorians became increasingly keen on *Death Portraiture*. What's that I hear you ask? Well, rather than summon the funeral director first and foremost - if one could afford it - the services of a funeral photographer would be called upon! Living family members were gathered to pose with their deceased loved one for a final photograph!

Most often, the bodies would be propped upright. Occasionally, fresh open eyes would be painted on to the photograph afterwards, obviously in an attempt to make it appear that the deceased person was still alive!

I've often wondered why the Victorians never smiled in photographs?

Was it perhaps that the dead person would have been the only one in the picture incapable of smiling?

The child on the left in the photograph below is the dead one!

Attributed to the Ann Longmore Etheridge collection

Moving on to Highgate…

13

FROM METROPOLIS TO NECROPOLIS

NEVER WOULD I have thought to describe a trip to a cemetery as a 'must do', but trust me when I say, any trip to London should include a visit to Highgate Cemetery!

If you are wowed by Gothic Horror films (which I am not) and/or, are an avid reader of Gothic Fiction, and furthermore, adore Gothic architecture, you will love it! It's a cemetery like no other! It really is atmospheric. Read the reviews on TripAdvisor if you doubt me. If you want to get a 'virtual' feel for the place watch *A Walk Around Haunted Highgate by Della Farrant* on YouTube to get a feel for it.

The thing that most struck me when we walked through the Cemetery was its wildness. Ivy rampages throughout. It wraps its tendrils around tombstones, and climbs up incredible monuments. Many ornate structures were commissioned by the wealthy to commemorate the passing of deceased loved ones, now slumbering peacefully (one hopes!) below ground. Dilapidated, lop-sided crumbling headstones, sit crooked amid the virulent plants that smother all that falls in their path.

The hauntings of Highgate West Cemetery, appear in the form of two different, yet vaguely (visually to some) similar manifestations. The first reveals itself as a black mist that evolves into an extraordinarily tall elongated black mass. I note some describe it as an 'elemental' haunting, so in effect - not a person as such, more a force. Truth to tell, it is not a pleasant entity to encounter! And I say this in all seriousness.

An extraordinary number of people have observed this phenomenon over the centuries, yet no one has ever been able to describe a face – in effect it is faceless. Many describe an entity which materialises wearing a conical hood – vaguely reminiscent of a cowled monk. There were never any monasteries in this area, so any phantom monk is ruled out.

It is malevolent. Those who dabble in witchcraft describe it as chthonic – deriving from the underworld - some ancient ancestral energy. This all sounds very 'deep', does it not! To my mind at least, wheresoever it origins lie is of little importance – the fact that it is negatively aggressive, is enough to scare the hell out of me!

Some describe it as having a hypnotic effect. Witnesses, having seen it, found themselves quite literally rooted to the spot on which they stood. Transfixed, they were unable to run away from it.

Two notable places it appears are inside the West Cemetery at the North Gate, and outside the boundary wall in Swains Lane. Swains Lane runs between Highgate's two cemeteries.

An Army Captain out walking his dog one night in Swains Lane, described the mass as something resembling black treacle that slowly slithered over the perimeter wall. Gradually it took on the form I have described. Both he and his dog were petrified. So distressed was the dog, it died a few days later. The dog had no pre-existing health problems!

Swains Lane

On one occasion, in 1965, the black mass ventured further afield, rising up to the third floor of a nearby Youth Hostel that overlooked the West Cemetery. It proceeded then to drift through the glass and into the building – not once, but on two different days! The young gentleman who first witnessed it, hadn't long moved into the area and had no prior knowledge of the phenomenon. He fled from the kitchen. Fellow residents mocked him when he described what had happened – until, that was, the following week. The entity chose to return, entering the property at exactly the same place, via the communal kitchen window. This time it was in full view of six witnesses. I know this all sounds very far-fetched, but there are disturbing things at play in Highgate itself, and there have been for a great deal of time.

Several private properties in the village of Highgate, have over the years, been haunted by something described as a *black mass*, one that has caused destruction and distress to the properties poor occupants.

Swains Lane (only a few yards from, and to the left of North Gate)

Note the eel shaped mist bottom left and again, inside the cemetery.
Both photographs courtesy of Redmond McWilliams.

The second regularly witnessed apparition is that of a man in a tall hat, dressed in a cloak. He makes no attempt to speak to people that have encountered him, but I would mention one incident on a night back in 1996. A lady taxi driver who was new to the area and unaware of Highgate's historic hauntings, was hailed down by the gent in question. His hand gesture was of a beckoning nature. Having now pulled up beside him, she asked if he required a lift. He didn't answer, but he did – wait for it – move closer with his hand held out, still coaxing her to come forth. Now, I can guarantee you - never would I have done what she did next, she started to get out of the taxi! However, having only partly done so, common sense kicked in. Feeling ill-at-ease to say the very least – she hastily got back in and drove off. She looked back through the rear view mirror, only to see he had quite literally vanished. The lane is exceptionally narrow and straight; therefore he would have been easily distinguishable had he been there.

Ghost tours of Highgate Cemetery are a regular event. But imagine the shock, on one such tour when five visitors asked if they always used live actors to impersonate the ghosts. The guide was rather alarmed to hear the question asked, and replied that they did not. Briskly steering them away from North Gate, she asked the group after the tour had ended, what they had seen. They described a man in a sweeping cloak, advancing towards them, before disappearing.

In addition, a mad old woman with long wild hair haunts East Cemetery. She's spotted frantically darting between headstones as if looking for something or someone. Many assume it to be the mother who murdered her two children. The body of one of the dead children was found by boys playing hide and seek. They found it hidden in a tree stump, within the Cemetery grounds.

If your camera fails you, as is so often the case in a haunted environment - yours will not be the first to have done so. One tutor took a college photography field trip to the Cemetery. One by one camera shutters jammed, batteries drained. Only one person managed to obtain a few photographs, which when developed revealed an expressionless old lady. Obviously she hadn't been there in person to pose for the cameras.

Highgate Cemetery was used regularly in the 1960s to film the *Hammer House of Horror* movies. And to be honest never was a place better suited to it! It has also been used as a film set for current day films such as *Fantastic Beasts*; *Dorian Grey*; *The Crimes of Grindelwald*.

Filming stories about Vampires proved problematic to say the least for Highgate residents, and in turn to Highgate Cemetery, to the extent that it was closed in 1975 for some considerable time.

Two groups, often seemingly unable to distinguish between fact and fiction, started to invade the place each night. Arguably, the lesser of these groups were the crazy teenagers, eager to view the black mass that some people had perceived to be a vampire. Up to 100 people a night would descend on the Cemetery, climbing over the gates, proceeding next to vandalising the area.

The other, more disturbing group, were those practicing black magic in the cemetery's vaults and flat areas. Animals were found, drained of blood, when ground-staff arrived to work the next day. Tell-tale chalked triangles and tools related to the practice were other indications that witches covens were at play.

Having long since ceased to be a profit-making venture - the most sought after plots taken up, and share-holders not having been paid dividends, the Cemetery eventually fell into a sorry and neglected state.

Highgate Cemetery has over 53,000 graves which accommodates more than 170,000 dead corpses. That's a lot of dead people!

It is the final resting place of a cross-section of famous people spanning decade after decade. Karl Marx; George Michael; Roger Lloyd-Pack (*actor in Only Fools and Horses*). Both parents of Charles Dickens, George Elliot, Michael Benting, Christina Rossetti. I could go on and on...

West Cemetery was opened in 1839. East Cemetery later in 1860. I see that East Cemetery is nearly full to capacity and looking for public support to expand and maintain it.

Check out Highgate Cemetery's website to book a tour, and see for yourself the wealth bestowed upon its tombs and famous Beer Mausoleum. You will be astounded.

Whilst you are up in Highgate, you might wish to later join in a Haunted Pubs tour from Highgate to neighbouring Hampstead. Hampstead is home to many celebrities, and the wealthiest in Britain's society. There are a number of groups running the pub walk. As always, check out the Internet for more details.

Hampstead really is quite lovely. If I could afford to live there, I would! It's like stepping back in time!

Both Highgate and Hampstead are easily accessible by either tube or bus from the city centre.

Della Farrant's book *Haunted Highgate* is an excellent read in which to learn more of Highgate's plethora of public and private residential hauntings.

Highgate Cemetery Catacombs
All Courtesy Wikipedia commons

Eastgate Cemetery
Attributed to Panyd

Highgate Cemetery Egyptian Avenue
Attributed to John Armagh

14

DEMON DOLLS &
POLTERGEIST PUPPETS

A chapter dedicated to Jean Evans

Courtesy of Russ Taylor

I AM QUITE aghast. Whilst researching material for this book, I have stumbled upon the strangest of hauntings. The first being a haunted doll. Apparently, there is more than one. In fact, there are several! There are no fewer than 150 of the dreaded things currently for sale on *eBay*. Heaven forbid! This particular doll, named '*Harold*' is world famous, and has an extensive life history. Purchased by his current owner in 2004 on *eBay*, he soon became, shall we say '*a problem*' to his owner, and thus was housed, with a dubious degree of safety, in a cupboard. I can hardly believe I am writing any of this? It is astonishing.

Now whether you believe things to be jinxed – possessed – cursed - whether you consider items carry with them bad omens - or even lucky ones - is a matter of opinion. The overriding problem with this doll is - it has a long association of bad things happening to its owners, their extended family and friends. Coincidental, or not? Well, that is for you to decide. But I can tell you, after the owner chose to bring Harold out of the closet, in order for hired paranormal investigators to get to know more of the little fella, the lead investigator became immediately ill with headaches, severe back pain, and a feeling of being disorientated. This, apparently, is quite common with many who come into contact with the doll.

Frankly, I don't even want to look at one of these dolls - let alone risk bidding on it. Imagine accidently pressing the '*bid*' key, and purchasing the damn thing! So, the next time you spy one of those old dolls with 'lively eyes', either at a car boot sale, or sat in some glass case at the back of some dusty musty smelling antique shop - or even a charity shop, for goodness' sake, leave it there! I should add, its previous owner stored the doll in its own coffin! Advised by a 'man of the cloth' to burn it, the owners attempted to - on more than one occasion - but he is a doll not easily combustible, and though rather battered, he still remains intact. I would further add, he sold for a very healthy $700, apparently. I am still shuddering at the image of Harold. He's only too easy to find - he can be viewed on *YouTube*. If you are intrigued, take a look. I, for one, have no intention of purchasing an image of him for you to view, in fear of downloading something nasty, and I don't mean a computer virus! A fear of dolls is known as Pediophobia. I think I have now acquired it.

Actually, Harold made his presence known to me in a rather puzzling way. He simply appeared on my *Kindle* - quite literally. I was in the process of purchasing a *Daily Mail* newspaper, when up sprang an image of Harold on my screen, along with the opportunity to purchase a book about him, '*The Terrifying True Story of the World's Most Haunted Doll*', written by Anthony Quinata. Having read a sample of the book, I have to say it is intriguing, and the history of the doll is quite disturbing.

As if a doll were not enough to contend with, apparently there are haunted mirrors. This gets more and more crazy. Humour me a moment:

imagine, if you will, booking into a haunted hotel, and there given a room in which, of all things, hangs a haunted mirror, and discovering that downstairs, in Reception, sits a haunted doll. Furthermore, you may later make the acquaintance of the hotel's resident spook. Personally, I'd much rather not do any of these things.

Whilst on the subject of dolls, should you ever find yourself in Italy, in the adorable resort of Stresa, I would definitely recommend a visit to *Rocca Di Angera*, the puppet and doll museum located on Isola Madre, Lake Maggiore. It is some 36 years since I visited it with my mother. To this day, the building, and its marionettes housed within, remain distinct in my mind. It is, I have to say, fascinating, yet downright creepy. The island is beautiful!

Hopping across the border into Austria, then heading to Salzburg to the eleventh century *Hohensalszburg Castle*, further descending into the Prince's cellars, you will find a collection of marionettes from the iconic *Salzburg Marionette Theatre*. They are housed in two of the fortress' dark rooms accessed via a tunnel in the basement. The visit is described 'as a somewhat creepy experience' on *TripAdvisor*. You don't say! Entrance is free. Truth be told, you would have to pay me good money to enter!

Closer to home, whilst in London you can visit the *Puppet Collection* within the *V & A Museum*. Adding to the fun, you can watch a Victorian melodrama. It is an adaptation of a true story, the murder of Maria Marten – *'Murder in the Red Barn'*, illustrated by way of a puppet show. Has the world gone mad? Why would one wish to take children to see a play about a murder?

The *Victoria & Albert* also houses a superb doll collection. Some date back to the 1600s. Many ancient civilizations used puppets. Many were found in the Egyptian tombs. You'll be delighted to know whilst visiting *Dunster Castle* on your ghost tour, you can take in a doll museum. You will find it located in the High Street.

I note the *Daily Mail* online published an article back in 2015 about a haunted puppet! The puppet's previous owner claimed that the puppet had tried to strangle her, so she gave it away to someone far braver than me. Its new owner restrained it, within a glass case that was blessed with holy water. Its movements - for move it did apparently - were filmed for three months. This is all getting too ridiculous! Lastly, on this subject, I would say, if you are looking for a riveting ghost story, look no further than 'Dolly' by Susan Hill.

15

ISLE OF WIGHT

HAVING SPENT A night at Spitbank Fort, it is merely a short journey by ferry to the Isle of Wight (alternatively known as the 'Haunted Isle'), where you can find the most splendid museum - *Lilliput Doll and Toy Museum*, Brading, Isle of Wight PO36 0DJ.

You may be pleased to know that the curators of the museum tell me none of their dolls are known to be possessed. Visitors to the museum, have however, reported feeling inexplicably cold, whilst at the same time seeing a little old lady wearing a shawl and poke bonnet, walk through part of the building, simply then to disappear. An image of Madam Tussaud comes to mind.

I notice the BBC did a feature on Brading's waxwork museum. It has sadly closed since the broadcast. The waxwork figures in the original museum, however, were said to have given many visitors recurring nightmares. Looking at photographs of them I can understand why! They are brilliant, even so. It is reported one waxwork figure, that of Queen Victoria, was seen to actually breathe. It was also said the figure occasionally tapped its foot. I often wonder what became of the figures?

Venturing further on a southerly course you arrive at *Ventnor Botanic Gardens*, upon which once stood the old *Royal National Hospital*. The site which once housed the old Operating Theatre is the most paranormally active. Closed in 1964, the majority of the buildings were demolished without too much difficulty. On the other hand - the Operating Theatre was going nowhere any time soon! It took an inordinate amount of mechanical equipment to demolish it. During the attempts to do so - and having finally succeeded - all manner of activity was reported by local residents, culminating in the need for the area to be exorcized by clergy several times - to no avail, I might add. Dogs are reported to be agitated in this area. The temperature is always distinctly cooler.

Demolition and renovation workers that followed described feeling uneasy in the vicinity of the old Operating Theatre. During daylight hours - usually morning or late afternoon, many workmen reported seeing a girl around the age of ten in this area. Sobs, moans and groaning are described as noises often heard. I should perhaps mention the footprint of the theatre is located beneath the current car park. So, double-check the hand-brake is on before you leave the car! During the course of your visit the likelihood is that you might make the acquaintance of phantom nurses and/or gaunt, long-since deceased, sickly-looking patients strolling beside you, whilst you roam its beautiful gardens. Dick Van Dyke (he of *Chitty Chitty Bang Bang* fame) was so enthralled on hearing of, shall we call it - their 'spirit problems' related to the demolition of the building, he ran features about it on his radio channel back in America. The gardens are open on Hallowe'en for tours, whereupon you can visit places not ordinarily open to the public. Ghost tours are also run on other days throughout the year.

Not far away from here is Appuldurcombe House. Though now basically a shell-like structure, here the sound of a wailing baby can be heard. Likewise, despite there being no evidence of a child in the vicinity, you may be greeted by the sound of a laughing five-year-old boy at Freemantle Gate. Failing these two things, you might yet see the famous horseless carriage appear up the drive at speed, merely then to slowly disappear. An unnatural chilling silence then prevails, according to those who have seen it.

Heading westerly from Ventnor, located near the village of Niton, stands *St. Catherine's Lighthouse* - a hive of ghost activity. Footsteps can be heard, when no-one is within the building. Items move of their own accord, and more often than is helpful, then proceed to vanish. Three former lighthouse-keepers were killed here during an air raid in the Second World War. Is it they, perhaps, who haunt the lighthouse?

En route homeward bound, near Newchurch, make a trip to Knighton Gorges Manor - the 're-appearing house', where, on New Year's Eve you and many others can gather to witness the reappearance of this long-since burned-down manor. Cursed and riven with tragedy, it is uncanny how many former residents were either driven to commit suicide, or their children to meet with early deaths. The manor was intentionally torched to the ground in 1820 by its owner George Maurice Bisset, in order to prevent his daughter from inheriting it as she had married a clergyman whom her father disapproved of.

A number of spirits have been seen within the grounds, at the gates, and at the periphery, by the waterworks. Fear not if your camera equipment ceases to function! You will not - for whatever reason - be the first to have found it a problem. Ghost tours are held weekly.

Madame Tussaud Waxwork figure of Queen Victoria
Courtesy of Russ Taylor

16

STIRRINGS ON THE STAIRWAY

SO MANY GHOSTS seem to frequent the staircase in all manner of properties - why a staircase? Well, I for one have no idea - if anyone else has, I'd very much like to know. One such manifestation, haunting the stairway of her former home, is the deceased Duchess of Lauderdale, who inherited *Ham House* from her father in 1655. Wealthy in her own right, and renowned for being both extremely ambitious and ruthless, when encountered she isn't the most amiable of ghosts. Members of the *National Trust's* own staff, and visiting public, even up to the present day, relate deeds of a malicious nature. Dressed in black, the Duchess is frequently seen on the staircase.

Alarmingly, staff and visitors often feel they have been pushed as they descend the stairs. I can't imagine, for one moment, such a person being happy about having hundreds of people walking the rooms of her beloved home day after day. No wonder she goes to such lengths to dissuade folk from visiting!

Ham House has numerous *'cold spots'*. When a ghost manifests itself, one way or another, it must draw energy or heat in order to do so. This in turn causes sudden fluctuations of temperature, thus creating *'cold spots'*. These can be measured with the aid of electromagnetic flow meters. Having experienced a *'cold spot'*, I have to tell you, a meter isn't a necessity in order to tell you something strange is going on!

On more than the odd occasion, an inexplicable scent of roses is also often smelt, and the sound of footsteps are heard in areas of the house where no-one is present. The property is also in possession of a haunted mirror, which is situated on the ground floor. Many refuse to look into it – including *National Trust* volunteers! I'm not sure what it is they fear seeing? The most scary thing, to my mind, would be to see no reflection at all - not even your own! A dog, resembling the same one that is depicted in paintings within the property, is often seen running along the corridors of *Ham House*. It should be noted that no dogs are allowed in the property; therefore, the possibility of it being any 'living' one can be ruled out. *Ham House* is situated on the Thames, on the outskirts of Richmond. Whilst in London, you may wish to take a trip out via train or tube to visit both the house and gardens.

Not all ghosts are malicious creatures of habit. Reflecting back for a moment to *The Lion Hotel* in Shrewsbury, an elderly lady known as *The Grey Lady* also walks the stairway. There does seem to be many a *Grey Lady* the world over, I should add! Those who have seen her, describe her as exuding a calming presence - in short, she is not scary at all. That said, one night porter, having met her, handed in his notice the next morning. After reaching the bottom of the staircase, she leaves via an external wall. This is understandable, as there was once a door there that led onto the street. I wonder if anyone has ever noticed her on the street itself?

At the National Maritime Museum, Greenwich, situated in the *Queen's House* section, is to be found the *Tulip Staircase*. On Sunday 19th June 1966, the Reverend R W Hardy and his wife visited the building whilst on holiday. As all keen tourists do, they duly took photographs of the interior of the building. It was late in the day. When developed, one of the photographs showed an apparition on the staircase. Neither person had seen anyone on the staircase at the time the photograph was taken. In fact, the stairway had been roped off, preventing anyone from using it. The photographs were examined by experts, including those at *Kodak*, who found no evidence of tampering during development.

I would like at this point to thank Geraldine Charles, Archivist at the *Royal Museum - Greenwich*. It was she

The Tulip Staircase
Courtesy of Greenwich Museum

who brought to my attention that the photograph of the *Tulip Staircase* ghost shows not one image, as many presume, but in fact three. She quotes, '*Many people have misinterpreted the image as showing one person - there are three figures in the image. It does not show a single hooded figure. The 'head' is actually a shoulder. The arms are both left arms - so you are actually seeing a figure that appears three times moving quickly up the stairs.*'

A vigil and séance were held in 1967 by the infamous '*Ghost Club*'. Watches were synchronised, soft-soled footwear donned, notebooks and pencils at the ready - but nothing conclusive happened. Members of both the staff and public have reported seeing a lady on the stairs over the course of time. Presences do not always manifest themselves visually. Sometimes - as I related earlier - they are physically felt, smelled, sensed, or heard, as is the case at our next property.

Heading up to the far-off county of Yorkshire, we arrive at another *National Trust* property which has paranormal activity in bucketloads. If we thought the Duchess of Lauderdale was not the nicest of persons ever to have walked the earth, here we discover one who surpasses her with ease. She was indeed, a cruel, spiteful stepmother. If the walls of *Nunnington Hall* could talk, they would have a horrendous tale to tell.

Lady Nunnington was determined that, following her husband's death, her son rather than her step-son would inherit *Nunnington Hall*. Lady Nunnington had her step-son imprisoned in an attic room. He was fed only bread and water. Concerned her staff would attempt to come to the poor child's aid, Lady Nunnington crept light of foot around the hall, spying on her staff. Unbeknown to his mother, her son visited his half-brother in the attic, taking him food whenever possible. Later, the imprisoned child disappeared under suspicious circumstances. In a frantic search for his half-brother, Lady Nunnington's own son met with a fatal accident - falling from an upper window.

Lady Nunnington is condemned to roam the Hall, the ghost of a bereaved woman. The phantom swish of her silk dress can often be heard moving up and down the staircase, as the cloth meets with each stair. The rustle of her dress is also heard passing through the hallways and rooms. The death of her own child drove her to insanity. Is she looking for her own son, killed tragically due to her wickedness, or still spying on her staff - who knows?

Books fly across rooms, doors open and shut of their own accord. The voices of children whispering are prevalent, heard all over the building

- but especially in the attic. A black, shapeless mass has been seen by visitors staying at the Hall, passing through the walls of the *Panelled Room*. Heaven help the staff who work at this property! The only good news seems to be, most of the activity happens at night. *Nunnington Hall* is situated near York, and sits on the river Rye. A visit to *Nunnington takes* you back to the 1920s - a period when the home saw happier times. As to other haunted *National Trust* properties - well, I have devoted a whole chapter to them, and fascinating they are too!

Last, but by no means least, there is the infamous photograph of *The Brown Lady* of *Raynham Hall*. It was taken in late September 1936, by Captain Hubert Provand and his assistant. Both were professional and well-established photographers, working on behalf of *Country Life*. The eponymous lady is seen walking the staircase of the Hall. As is always the case, some questioned its validity. However, the negatives were examined, and in turn, were deemed to be genuine. Some still doubt its authenticity - but none have proved it to be a fake. Many a visitor to the Hall has seen this very recognisable lady in her brown brocade dress - the most famous being King George the fourth - who left immediately, declaring the building to be cursed! But who is she? The spirit in question is identified as Lady Dorothy Walpole. *Raynham Hall* is open to the public by prior appointment. Check the *Internet* for more details.

The Brown Lady
Courtesy of Wikipedia

17

NATIONAL TRUST
HAUNTED BUILDINGS

HAVING SPOKEN WITH the *National Trust*'s volunteers and guides about their 'other-worldly' experiences, I have come to the conclusion they are indeed the most courageous of folk! Also, that if you are an avid ghost hunter you will find no better opportunity to meet with one than to…

    A. Visit when the property is not busy.

    B. Falter at the end of a touring group at any of the *Trust's* properties listed in this chapter.

    C. Join as a volunteer, when you, in all probability, will be allocated a job in one of the 'occupied rooms'. During a period when the building is not open to the public, you are sure to experience hearing, feeling or seeing all manner of these things.

    D. If you are of a nervous disposition - do none of them!

Imagine – on a bleak winter's afternoon, when, without your realising it, the dark has crept upon the landscape by 3p.m.; only the odd visitor (if any) has passed through the premises. So quiet is it - save for the odd creaking floorboard - or slowly squeaking door hinge - one could hear a pin drop - and you are there – quite alone, as a *Trust* volunteer, in one of the dimly lit rooms or hallways, or so you thought!

Having paid a visit to *Nunnington Hall*, whilst you are in York, head on over to another *National Trust* property in which there are ghosts galore - *The Treasurer's House*. Its owner, *Frank Green*, bequeathed the building to the *National Trust* in the 1930s, vowing to haunt the building should any of his beloved collection be tampered with, moved or heaven forbid – REMOVED! So fanatical was he, even the floors were studded (the studs still visible for the public to see) in order to designate where various treasures should remain. Inevitably during time, the promise, to leave all as it once was, had to be broken. To preserve various items from exposure to sunlight, etcetera, some had to be moved, which made Frank a 'very unhappy chap'. Frank remained true to his word, and has caused much mayhem since.

Treasurer's House is also home to Roman Centurions - of the ghost variety. The House sits above a Roman road. Visit the basement exhibition room, where you can watch a video of an interview with Harry Martindale. Harry was an apprentice plumber in 1953. Aged 18, he was given the job of drilling a hole in the ceiling of the cellar to install a new central heating pipe. Having put his ladder on an excavated area of the Roman road, he set about his work. Not realising the enormity of the job (the walls in the cellar being several feet deep) it was on the second day of drilling, he heard a horn blowing. The sound seemed to come from within the wall. Following this, a horse and rider emerged from the wall (not a living one, obviously!). Petrified by the sight of this, he fell off his ladder, landing on his back in a corner. Before he could hot-foot it out of the cellar, there followed several ghostly foot soldiers, all of whom proceeded to march past him, then they disappeared through the opposite wall. Once he was sure all the grimy Roman soldiers had passed through, he fled. The curator of the Museum knew immediately what Harry had seen.

"By the look of you, you've just seen the Roman soldiers," he remarked unhelpfully. Harry was livid - no-one had forewarned him! He never returned to the cellar to complete the job. His doctor signed him off for two weeks – '*Suffering from shock'.*

Harry was persuaded to relate the experience for the DVD 'Ghosts of York' produced by Richard Felix. It is available to buy on *Amazon*. You can watch the interview too, filmed in the cellar itself, on the *Internet*. Type in his name, and log onto *Vimeo*.

Making a journey further north whilst in Yorkshire, we arrive at *Fountains Abbey*, where debatably - if you are lucky enough - you may be entertained by the 'singing monks' in the *Chapel of Nine Altars*. It all sounds rather wonderful, does it not - except for the fact they are all, long since dead and buried! Regardless of that, many have heard them, and very good they are too, apparently!

Another *National Trust* property where strange experiences have occurred is *Chartwell* in Kent, the former home from 1924 until his death, of Sir Winston Churchill. Churchill relates in an article entitled 'Dreams', that he was visited one dull afternoon in November by the ghost of his father - furthermore - that he had a long conversation with him. The inexplicable waft of cigar smoke lingers in the air on occasions, despite a non-smoking rule.

I'm not aware of anyone having seen the ghost of Churchill. The home remains much as it was when the family lived there. Much loved, and set in beautiful grounds, it is well worth a visit.

Heading off to another majestic landscape, with weather at times equally as harsh as that in Yorkshire, we must set the Sat Nav on a south westerly course to Wales. Welcome to *Newton House*, Dinefwr in Carmarthenshire. The House is set in a more tranquil part of Wales, in the Welsh valleys at their greenest and grandest. Here people have seen the *White Lady*, who simply vanishes into a cupboard. If, on visiting the property, you begin to feel a little short of breath, you will not be the first to have done so. Occasionally, visitors have reported the sensation of fingers gripping them around their throats. The figure dressed in white is said to be Lady Elinor Cavendish, who was murdered here. Not wanting to marry her suitor, she sought sanctuary in the House. He - in turn - incensed at having been rejected, on finding her, took it upon himself to strangle poor Elinor. Is it any wonder she wasn't keen on the chap? The scent of cigar smoke unexpectedly lingers in the air, despite a strict no smoking rule. Lights switch themselves on and off. Voices echo in empty rooms. As always in any haunted property, there are sudden unaccountable fluctuations in temperature.

Staying in Wales, we head to Welshpool, Powys. Sitting just over the Welsh/English border we arrive at *Powis Castle*; a lovely building, with beautiful terraced gardens, in which the proudest of peacocks roam. The *Clive Museum* is a must see here – it is rich in Indian treasures. It also has a deer park, and a piano that often plays by itself! Yes, *Powis Castle* is home to a phantom pianist! Staff have known the room to be empty - and more to the point - the doors to the ballroom wing locked, when a melody can be heard drifting throughout the Castle. I don't know about you, but I shudder at the thought of seeing the piano keys playing of their own accord. I am reminded once again of a scene from *'Phantom of the Opera'*, when such a thing happens. Some research mentions a gent in a gold suit putting in the odd appearance (possibly a reincarnation of Liberace? Now I am showing my age!)

Staff have often seen a lady in black, seated in a chair by the fireplace in the '*Dukes Room*'. Visitors have experienced being stroked on the arm. The staff working in the tearoom report their shirts being tugged, and the figure of a child dressed in green has been seen in the *Clive Museum*. Workmen have reported being touched on their necks when working on the staircase. Other than that, all is peaceful! Having visited it, I have to admit, I felt at ease and thoroughly enjoyed the visit and shall return. Situated in the garden, I should add, is a Georgian cottage which sleeps up to seven people. If you wish to spend a night there in the grounds of the castle, here is your opportunity. Contact the *National Trust* for details.

Perhaps having decided on a trip to Buckfastleigh (mentioned in the next chapter)'A Grave Matter', and/or whilst visiting Buckfastleigh's caves, you may also have the yearning to head further westward to *Buckland Abbey*, Yelverton, Devon. Situated on the edge of Dartmoor, it is the home of Sir Francis Drake and his '*horrible hounds of hell!*' It is said Sir Francis was not averse to the odd dabbling in black magic. The sound, apparently, from the beat of his Snare drum, is to be heard whenever England is threatened. Good for him I say! Any help is more than welcome.

Cider House and *Cider Cottage* stand in the Abbey estate. Both are *National Trust* owned, idyllic and available for those wishing to spend a night here. As always see the website for more details. Keep an ear open for the 'horrible hounds' and the drum of course!

Travelling north we arrive at *Dunster Castle*, near Minehead in Somerset. It stands tall and proud amongst trees on a hill. Such has been the enthusiasm by those on the 'other side' to scare staff and visitors witless, the Trust, as requested by staff, had the castle exorcised. The exorcism failed dismally! The *King Charles* bedroom is said to be the most haunted room. Its atmosphere is described as malevolent in the extreme.

In the *Leather Room* male voices are to be heard, and sudden temperature drops felt. Again, a distinct sense of unease has been experienced by many. The two most-observed ghosts are a guard wearing a tri corn hat and '*The Grey Lady*' (yes, another one) who is often seen walking – yes, you guessed correctly - down the staircase. Many skeletons were found in the dungeons, one, of a seven-foot manacled giant. Dogs refuse to walk down the steps leading to the dungeons. Petrified by what, we don't know, nor do a percentage of us even wish to. It seems like only yesterday that I visited Dunster and its Castle. Dunster is the most heavenly place. Quintessentially English, in essence adorable. Do go - you will immediately fall in love with it. And don't forget to visit the Dolls Museum!

Venturing from Somerset into Dorset, we arrive at *Corfe Castle*. Although a castle in ruins, much remains, standing mightily impressive. You can reach it by road, or take a boat from Bournemouth pier, or Poole, sailing around *Harry's Rocks*. Arriving in Swanage, it is but a mere 10 minutes' walk to the station. From here one can take a steam train ride to Corfe and the castle. Waiting to greet you at the bridge, on dark and gloomy nights, is the headless 'lady in white'.

Crossing the country we head east to Norfolk, where, residing in *Felbrigg Hall*, is the ghost of a man after my own heart. William Windham was infatuated by books, and an avid collector of them. Trying in vain to save books from his burning library, sadly, he perished in the fire. He is a regular user of his library even to this day, returning when a precise collection of books is placed upon the table - but which are they? I hate it when they tell only half the tale!

By all accounts, the whole family throughout the generations were somewhat eccentric, to say the least. It's worth a visit simply to see the Gothic Library, and to read more of the family and of their quirky existence, and perhaps wander over to *Felbrigg Church*. Some of the Windham coffins are in the crypt for all to see. How nice!

Turning west to the Midlands, we come to a moated manor house, *Baddesley Clinton*, located in Warwickshire. A fascinating place to visit, not just for its spirit occupants, but for the sheer number of priest holes, ingeniously located in the most unusual of places. There is also a scandalous tale to be told. On returning home unexpectedly, Sir Nicholas Brome found his wife and the local priest in a compromising position. Tales vary as to how compromising. Sir Nicolas, not happy at this, immediately stabbed the priest. Having remarkably escaped a murder charge, as penance for taking the priest's life, he paid for extensive work on the nearby Parish Church of St. Michael to be carried out. Servants and guests to the house have witnessed door handles turning of their own accord. Footsteps have been heard along corridors when no other person has been present. Written diary evidence from previous guests supports this.

Having programmed the Satellite Navigation to our last destination, the immediate instruction (to my mind at least) should be '*Turn around as soon as possible!'.* Saving possibly, the eeriest until last, we arrive at *Speke Hall* in Liverpool, a Tudor mansion located on the banks of the Mersey. A place of much unrest, the Hall is saturated by presences - and not one of them friendly! Unexplained dark shadows are often seen hovering around the *Great Hall.* Staff and guests describe the room as having an oppressive and deeply morose feel to it. Many too, have felt suddenly nauseous on entering it.

In the *Blue Room* lurk more dark shadows, but by far worse, the words *"Get out!"* have been heard, issued by way of a hissing whisper.

Footsteps have been heard in the upper corridors when the Hall is closed to the public. Children crying is a regular occurance. Our final apparition at *Speke Hall* is that of a woman who walks the *Tapestry Room.* The story is that Mary Norris threw her child out of an upper window, then proceeded to follow him. It is supposed it is she, along with the wails of the child, that account for these occurrences, I suppose we'll never know? One can join guides at 6.30pm in the *Great Hall* for more ghostly tales in this turbulent Tudor black and white building. See the *National Trust* website for more details on all these properties.

I'm certain many more of the *Trust* properties have a tale to tell. As much as I admire the *Trust* for their outstanding work, I do baulk at having to pay additional exorbitant prices, at every given opportunity they find, in which to extract money from me. I am certain, if the opportunity arose, whereby they were able to charge me for the dubious pleasure of seeing the odd apparition, they would indeed, do just that.

Chartwell – Home of Winston Churchill
Courtesy of Russ Taylor

Winston Churchill
Courtesy of Russ Taylor

Corfe Castle
Courtesy of Russ Taylor

18

A GRAVE MATTER

Hound of The Baskervilles
Artist S Paget

SIR ARTHUR CONAN Doyle's novel *'The Hound of the Baskervilles'*
was inspired by the story of a living person - Squire Richard Cabell.
Cabell was a man with a passion for hunting. Many considered he led an
immoral lifestyle - and in turn - it was said - he had sold his soul to the
devil. Those who knew him, described him as someone both monstrous
and evil. Had he lived on the English/Welsh border his family might
well have employed one of our *Sin-Eaters* to attend his funeral! He died
in 1677.

Legend has it that, in a fit of rage, he murdered his wife. In turn, her
devoted hound then attacked and killed him! As is often the case, the
tale varies, but the common denominator of the story is that upon the
night of his burial a pack of baying ghostly hounds came from across the

moor - the terminus of their journey being the Cabell tomb. So terrified were the villagers they built a prison-like cell surrounding the grave. Their aim was to prevent his spirit from escaping, and furthermore, to ensure that he and the *'horrible hounds'* could never roam the moors. Neither did it stop at that: over his tombstone, a stone altar slab was laid on top of the tomb itself. The structure has bars at its front, a slate pitched roof, and a heavy wooden back door. It rather reminds me of a cross between a 1950s bus shelter, and a lay-by cafe. Should the whim take you, it can still be viewed to this day in Buckfastleigh churchyard. It is truly hideous. On stormy nights the hounds are said to return to the imprisoned tomb.

The church itself has suffered two attacks by arsonists, once in Victorian times, and again in 1992. Its spire has been struck by lightning. The Second World War saw its stained-glass windows shattered. It now stands, an empty shell. It is rumoured to be a 'Mecca' for devil-worshipping groups, given its link to our evil Squire Cabell.

Sir Arthur Conan Doyle, fascinated by the stories of the hounds, toured Devon and Dartmoor. He visited the sepulchre, amongst other places, absorbing the atmosphere of this often tempestuous, turbulent, desolate landscape, with its lethal mires and dense fogs, which, on a seemingly serene and beautiful day, have been known to envelop the moor within 20 minutes.

Sir Arthur toured the moors with a friend. Their driver's name was Harry Baskerville. Sir Arthur liked the surname immensely, and with the driver's permission, used it to create the fictional Baskerville family and Baskerville Hall, the centre of the plot. Another Devon folklore tale mentions *The Yeth Hound* - is it one and the same creature? It is described as a headless hound - the spirit of an unbaptized child.

A myriad of caves runs below the tomb of the Cabell family; one stretch leads from the church to the Cabell tomb. Directly underneath the tomb a stalagmite and stalactite have joined together, resembling the shape of a man. Despite the villagers' best efforts, might the Squire have escaped via the basement, and now be reincarnated in this form?

Should you wish to explore the caves, look up *Pengelly Caves*, Buckfastleigh, on the *Internet* for more details. Incidentally, the caves are home to many Greater Horseshoe bats - approximately 1,200 at the last count. As the sun sets, should you stand on the steps of the church, you will probably see them take flight. Not wishing to risk hearing the hounds, furthermore, neither wanting to have 1,200 bats swooping down on me, I think I shall give that a miss, and set off to the hotel for dinner instead! Point to note – any Conan Doyle fans, may wish to take in the *Sherlock Holmes Museum*, Baker Street, London, NW1 6XE.

For the most bizarre reasons, things often happen which defy logical explanation, but on occasions a possible reason, given time, comes to light. A tree once grew in London's *Green Park*, known by locals as *The Ghost, or Death Tree*. For whatever reason, many had chosen to end their days, opting to hang themselves from its branches. The tree is long since gone, yet it is said, there is still an ominous presence where it once stood. Tramps and vagabonds still avoid the area where the tree was situated.

Animals, uninfluenced obviously by stories, seem uncannily perceptive about such things, and are unhappy to be in certain locations, as is the case regarding this tree. Birds, it is said, never rested in its branches; neither did wildflowers grow in the park. *Green Park*, once swampland, was used by *St James' Hospital* to bury patients who had died of leprosy. Is this the reason why flowers do not readily grow here? Well, whoever knows? I can report, though, on a beautiful sunlit day, after many hours walking the streets of London, I slept like a baby upon its grass. Little did I know I was sleeping upon a mass burial site!

Only a few weeks ago a news item came on T.V. Two skeletons had been discovered in a suburban household garden. The family had always been perplexed as to why nothing would ever grow in this section of it. The conclusion of the story was that the two skeletons were in fact linked to an unsolved murder case. What an awful discovery to make!

19

NORTH WEST BOUND

HAVING JOURNEYED NORTH west to the previously mentioned *Speke Hall*, you might wish to stay a little longer, taking in a few more places of interest. A grade two listed building awaits, offering *'Dusk till Dawn'* stays, in a derelict hospital. Over the years the building has served as an orphanage, old peoples' home and a mental asylum. *Newsham Park Hospital* (see photographs) built in 1870, is located on Orphan Lane. Well, of all the places I have come upon, this is by far the worst place imaginable in which to spend any time whatsoever, let alone to hold a nightly vigil! Hand on heart, I have to say, lives of my nearest and dearest would have to depend upon my merely stepping foot inside the place - let alone spending a night in it!

From the outset, its appearance stirs within me a deep sense of unease, suggestive of sinister things having occurred inside. Depressingly surrounded by wire fencing, its windows boarded up, it presents a melancholy sight.

Ignoring its dismal décor of blistered peeling paintwork, and tattered wallpapers - stepping into the dark corridors - through a debris of discarded hospital trollies, and abandoned wheelchairs - a feeling of foreboding surges within you. Looking up to the decrepit staircases, you will note the banisters are guarded with anti-suicide grilles! A more morbid building I cannot imagine!

With much trepidation, treading cautiously up the desolate stairways to the upper floors, you will come to - of all things - the mortuary – still complete with fridges - thankfully empty of corpses! Empty wards with deserted beds in-situ remain in the building. There is a chapel, bell tower, and a school, all housed within the building, so you can imagine the sheer size of this stark place.

A former hospital worker, Mr John Gray, interviewed by the Liverpool Echo (which can be viewed on the Internet) declares the building should have been demolished, such is the evil prevalent within it. There are harrowing stories to be heard. Seriously why would you even want to go? Many do though - paying good money for the experience! You may even be one of them!

The place is vast. With an underground warren of basement rooms and corridors, ghosts are regularly seen darting out of sight. Voices are heard echoing down through the corridors. Tools temporarily laid down by workmen, reappear in the most bizarre places - some a considerable distance from where they were originally placed.

Before commencing on a ghost hunting tour in 2017, I came upon a report in the *Sun* newspaper, which included a photograph of a group of enthusiasts. Posted on *Facebook* the next day - clearly visible, could be seen, an additional member of the party, centre of picture, who wasn't there in person at the time the photograph was taken. Check it out on the *Internet*, it's very creepy!

If you decide to go, I wish you well. Take all the amulets you possess with you. Tea, coffee and biscuits are free of charge. Organisers advise it is extremely cold, so wear your thermals.

Two episodes in the *'Britain's Most Haunted'* TV show, presented by Yvette Fielding and the team, featured two properties in Cheshire. The first, *Capesthorne Hall* in Macclesfield. It is currently running as a prestigious wedding venue. Severed limbs that open windows, ghostly shapes descending the stairs of the chapel vault and the usual grey lady, are on the list of the day's activities to be viewed here. The second, *Tatton Park Old Hall*, is owned by The National Trust. HH & Spooky Nights website is where to head to book your nightly ghost vigil. Good luck! You'll need it, having watched the episode. The most ardent investigators, have been petrified witless, exploring the dark recesses of this seriously sinister building! I should further warn you, if you are female, beware - one of the ghosts is a drunken male. He is physically abusive towards women visitors, and very active! Neither forget to visit Tatton Park Mansion (situated on the same site). Besides an array of ghostly females, haunting the property, the episode exploring the mansion revealed the sound of ghostly dogs. The most intriguing (to me at least) was the sudden swinging of two different ladles hung in the kitchen. No one was stood anywhere near the ladles at the time. Having been steadied by one of the team members, off they went again – not swinging merrily back and forth, but more oddly, one of the two ladles swung in a pendulum motion, from side to side. Eventually one ladle flew across the room, narrowly missing one of the investigating female team members.

Newsham Park Hospital
Attributed to Phil Nash Wikipedia commons

Tatton Park Old Hall
Attributed to Peter I Vardy

20

FURTHER NORTHERLY BOUND

HAVING VISITED BOTH *Fountains Abbey* and *Nunnington Hall*, why not book into the Grade 2 listed Unicorn Hotel, located in the idyllic cathedral city of Ripon, North Yorkshire. The *Unicorn* is haunted by one Tom Crudd, nick-named 'Old Boots'. He was employed as boot boy at the coaching inn. Possessing an extraordinarily long nose and chin, so long in fact, he could hold a coin between his lip and chin; he was often tipped, by passing travellers, simply for performing this trick. Tom - I should add - is still often seen. Vintage brass door knockers, modelled on Tom Crudd, produced around the 1900s, can be found for sale occasionally in antique shops, etc. Looking at images of him, his chin and nose together form more the shape of a beak. The door knocker depicts him carrying the customary slippers (as he would have done) for arriving guests, along with a bootjack. On the reverse side of some knockers can be found an engraving of his tombstone! A ghostly child has also been seen looking down from an upper window of the hotel. Let's hope it's less noisy than those at the *Georgian House Hotel* in London - if you've a mind to stay there. Its reviews, I should mention, are splendid, as are those of Ripon itself.

Most strangely, the clergymen of Ripon are a body of people with the power to execute anyone if they feel the need. So - whilst there - don't upset the vicar! The Cathedral is supposedly lovely. Drop a £5 note in the collection box, and all should be well.

Ripon has an abundance of places with a story to tell. Its *Victorian Workhouse Museum* is home to 'Gordon', a former employee of the building. Many tourists have been welcomed by him, despite the fact Gordon has long since passed away. He isn't the only ghost present. The building has been another that the *Britain's Most Haunted* team have visited. During the filming the crew contacted a child (Henry) through a Ouija-styled board. The instruction to spirits present was to knock when the investigator's finger fell upon the letter needed to spell out their name. On this occasion, it spelled out the name of a five-year-old boy. Risking being called a killjoy, I cannot help but wonder, would a five-year-old orphan of the 1800s even be able to write, let alone know how to spell his name? Personally, I don't think so. That said, I strongly recommend you do not succumb to the temptations of the Ouija board. In fact, there is a short chapter dedicated to the dangers of them.

Ripon's other haunted abode is the *Prison and Police Museum*. (See the Internet for opening times of both museums.) Opened in 1686, it was known as a *House of Correction for Vagrants*. In 1816 it became a jail, renamed Liberty Prison. It ended its days as a police station in 1956. Continuing investigations, *Britain's Most Haunted* transferred to this museum, where the crew encountered problems with batteries draining from lighting in no time whatsoever, and cameras unaccountably failing. It is reportedly haunted by former inmates, and a prison officer. Keys are heard turning in a lock. A bell rings on a policeman's bicycle when no one is in the vicinity. Voices echo in the corridors and cells. It is a riveting visit, by all accounts, whether you are a 'believer, or a non-believer' in ghosts.

Fountains Abbey Mentioned in chapter 17
Attributed to Dr Moschi

21

SOUTH WEST BOUND

SHOULD YOU HAVE chosen, instead of Ripon, to head south-west, deciding to view *Buckfastleigh* and *Buckland Abbey*, as mentioned in previous chapters, or en route to Cornwall, a reservation at the infamous *Jamaica Inn* immediately springs to mind. On visiting the inn, Daphne du Maurier was captivated by it, going on to live there, and write the famous book of the same name. There have been several film adaptations of the book - Alfred Hitchcock's being one. It was apparently rated his worst film. What a shame he didn't do justice to such a dark, tempestuous story! *Jamaica Inn* is not only a hotel, but also home to the *Smugglers Museum*, with tales to be told of murders, the smuggling of contraband, ship wreckers and piracy. Novelist Alistair Maclean, the author of spy thrillers such as *The Guns of Navarone* and *Where Eagles Dare*, was also a former owner of *Jamaica Inn*. At the point of reading all about *Jamaica Inn*, I discovered it, too, had featured in *Britain's Most Haunted*, and was the focus of other Ghost Societies' investigations. It was, and continues to be, described as one of the creepiest properties they have thus far investigated. Bedroom 4 is the one to reserve for an extraordinary experience. Take a drink in the *Stable* or *Smugglers' Bar*, where a great deal of paranormal activity has been witnessed, along with its restaurant!

In Room 5, a haunted mirror hangs on the wall. On looking into the mirror, the faces of a mother and baby have been witnessed staring back! Many managers over the years have heard voices - conversations in a foreign language, possibly Celtic. You may also meet with a gent in a cloak, who appears able to walk through wooden doors. By the way, he is apparently of a somewhat malevolent nature - so best let him go first!

Having had an entertaining night at *Jamaica Inn*, you may choose to head to *Bodmin Jail*, where you can spend the night incarcerated, so long as you are over the age of 18. Why anyone would want to do such a thing is beyond me - but each to their own. I have visited it during the hours of daylight. Just looking at it from afar fills you with a sense of ominous dread, even before descending into the dark and sinister interior of the place. It is extraordinarily atmospheric, sending shivers down your spine on the balmiest of days. It was built in 1779.

Prideaux Place, near Padstow, is an Elizabethan manor house. It is open to visitors *(see opening times on their website)*. You may meet with the spirit of a boy in the kitchen, a woman sewing in the morning room, or a lady, Honor Fortescue, who chose to throw herself off the upper balcony after the death of her husband. Some say she was pushed.

A visit worth doing if you are a keen 'ghostbuster' is the *Ram Inn* in Wotton Under Edge, Gloucestershire. Yes - once again – it is a place investigated by many of the societies devoted to seeking the little ghostly blighters out. The inn is supposedly teeming with the most ghastly of them. The once Bishop of Gloucester, the Rt Reverend John Yates, tried in vain to exorcise the inn, and was quoted as saying it was the most evil place he had ever had the misfortune to visit. Owned by a family who apparently, quote, 'embrace the hauntings', it is available at a mere £69 a night, to spend a vigil in. Go to the *Haunted Rooms* website, should a visit appeal.

Prideux Place Courtesy of Olaf Tausch

You will appreciate there are quite literally hundreds of places worth a mention, located all around Britain. There are many more roads on which to travel in search of them.

Bodmin Jail
By Chris j wood - Own work, CC BY-SA 3.0, http

22

SPOOKY BLINDERS!

VIRTUALLY EVERY PLACE mentioned in previous chapters, and others yet to follow, are reachable from *Birmingham Railway Station*. Should you ever find yourself in *New Street Station* you might be questionably 'fortunate' enough to spy a ghost or two. Platform 4 sits directly above a Jewish Cemetery. The cemetery was somewhat insensitively bulldozed, then dug up, to make way for a new line! Following this, an extraordinary amount of suicides have been committed on this platform.

For instance, Walter Hartles, a former railway worker, took his life one lonely night, by shooting himself in the face whilst sitting in the waiting room. You might well find yourself sat alongside him whilst awaiting the arrival of your train.

Also on Platform 4, Claude, another gent worth looking out for. He chose to poison himself. He's pretty easy to identify as he appears dressed in Victorian costume. Tragedy also struck the platform in 1921, a train crash killing three, with many others sustaining injuries.

You need travel no further afield than Birmingham to visit the *Catacombs* - located in the Jewellery Quarter, in Warstone Lane Cemetery (B18 6NN). The catacombs date back to 1847, and are home to a few ghosts – one of a woman dressed in 1930s attire. Witnesses have seen her pass through walls, and even a parked car! On occasions, a familiar smell reminiscent of pear drops accompanies her. It is assumed, this is, in fact, the scent of potassium cyanide - which was, at one time, used in gold and silver plating. Did the poor lady die from cyanide poisoning? A 'White Lady' is also seen in the cemetery, and on the road outside the perimeter of the site. The other ghost is that of a young woman who is seen at night, sitting on her own grave.

Having viewed the *Catacombs*, you might wish to visit another intriguing place. I would at this point, like to acknowledge Sarah Hayes - The Coffin Works and Museum Manager. The *Coffin Works* is one of many museums based in the Jewellery Quarter. Newman Brothers manufactured most things to do with coffins - save for the coffin itself. Newman Brothers produced the finest burnished brass coffin handles money could buy, from 1894 until 1998, affordable only to the upper-classes, church nobility and royalty. It now operates as a fascinating museum by day – but if you are up for yet another thrilling night, you might wish to spend a nightly vigil there. It is home to a ghostly night watchman - often seen at the factory windows – despite - obviously – the building being empty! Check out the *Haunted Evenings* website, including the words *Coffin Works*. A nightly vigil, as at June 2020, costs £40. It includes the use of all manner of experimentational tools.

With stylish restaurants and cafes, the Jewellery Quarter is also a good place to head for lunch. Check out *TripAdvisor* for more details of the cemetery and the Coffin Works Museum opening times.

As in London, Birmingham's theatres are also a hive of activity of the ghostly variety. The *New Alexandra Theatre* (commonly known as the *Alex*) is located on Station Street. One former owner - Leon Salberg - is one ghost still roaming the theatre. Is he possibly still overseeing proceedings? In fact, the theatre has a somewhat ghostly payroll. A former Master of the Wardrobe Department also haunts the place. A Stage Manager named Dick likes to make his presence known by jangling keys. There is also a man in a military hat – and yet another 'Grey Lady'. As I mentioned previously, a few actors have died on stage - Arthur Lowe (Captain Mainwaring as he is fondly known to many) didn't do anything quite so dramatic as to die during his performance – but did die in his dressing-room at the Alex. Backstage tours are available.

I note, there have in the past been 'lock-in' ghost tours if you are of that persuasion - as is also the case at Birmingham's *Steelhouse Lane Police Station*. For 126 years, gangsters and serial killers were held in this Victorian building. I am shaking my head once again – why would anyone want to spend a night in the cells! Many, far braver than me, do though! Check out *Steelhouse Lane Police Station's* ghost hunts - *HH & Spooky Nights* website.

Another tour run by the same company is one held at a secret (or at least it once was) nuclear bunker. Situated near Kinver, Kidderminster - approximately 17 miles from Birmingham - *Drakelow Tunnels* were originally constructed between 1941-42. The car manufacturer Rover used the site as a shadow factory to manufacture parts for aircraft engines. In 1961 the underground area was designated a nuclear bunker. Further work, carried out in the 1980s, ensured safety in the event of an attack. The M.O.D. decommissioned the site in 1993. A great deal of information about the tunnels is still protected by the *Official Secrets Act*.

More than three miles of tunnels await you. You can watch previous explorations of the tunnels on *YouTube*. The digital channel *Really* is well worth watching for the interviews with people who have no desire to return to the site! As was the case at Fan Bay, the history of them is quite fascinating. Tunnels 1 and 4 see the most paranormal activity. I would finally add, security guard dogs refused to return into the tunnels, having been totally spooked by whatever exists inside! The ratings of the tours on *TripAdvisor* are excellent. The tunnels are extremely cold – so wrap up warm!

For those of us who like a touch of luxury, you will find nowhere better than the following places to lay your head after a day touring the area. Whether you find the night to be without 'activity' is another matter! *Ettington Park Hotel* is one place worth mentioning. A Neo-Gothic architecture building - described as the most haunted hotel in England! The hotel was used for the 1963 film *The Haunting*. Filmed in black and white, it somehow makes it even more eerie than if it had been made in colour. The hotel in the film is renamed Hill House. I've watched the trailer on the Internet (as can you) it looks terrifying to me.

To be honest it's easier to list areas in the hotel that aren't haunted, for there is an abundance of ghosts residing here! Objects move by themselves on a regular basis. Voices (not of the living) are heard somehow drifting in the area around people. Shadows dart across rooms and hallways, and objects levitate. Such is the amount of spirit activity in Room 6, an emergency cord has been installed! And it's not for those who have merely had an accident! Neither is it probably best to head to the Stour Corridor on your own – for you - more than likely - will find you are indeed - not on your own! Two children who drowned in the river Stour around 1800 are regular visitors to it. They don't limit their activities to just this area – they have been experienced throughout the hotel. Accompanying them in the corridor is the apparition of a monk, and yet another 'Grey Lady'. A young servant girl named Mary haunts both the main staircase and the *Oak Room Restaurant*. Pushed from the stairs by her master, she died in the fall.

At the last count there have been no less than twenty-one other apparitions; they include an Edwardian lady seen walking bare-footed. The architect of the building itself - John Prichard - and a previous groundsman are two other ghosts - plus one other child, who hovers elsewhere...I could go on, and on. Much better to visit it and see for yourself! It has excellent reviews.

Continuing on the luxurious front – why not book either the *Peacock* or *Rose Suite* in *Warwick Castle*. It is built upon an even older fortification. The Castle was built by William the Conqueror – is it any wonder it's haunted? I was on the point of booking the *Peacock* or *Rose* suites in *Warwick Castle* - but having read more of its ghosts, now I'm not so sure! The suites do look exceptional, though! They are located in the *Caesar's Tower*. The price (around £600 a night) includes a private tour of the Castle and dungeons with a guide. You also have two days to view the Castle, its dungeons and grounds independently, should you so wish. Champagne and breakfast is also included in the price. It mentions the dungeons may not be suitable for children under 10 – nor for me - having been given the low-down on the resident phantom haunting them. He sounds most horrid! He is, apparently, somewhat similar to the malicious one residing at the *Prince Rupert Hotel* in Shrewsbury. He attacks visitors, literally scratching them, screaming 'Get out!' He was known in life to have been a sadistic torturer of his prisoners, gaining much pleasure on the way.

Sir Fulke Greville haunts the *Watergate Tower*. He is seen so regularly it is now known as the *Ghost Tower*.

Stories vary as to the true identity of Moll Bloxham. We do know she lived within the Castle grounds, selling milk and dairy produce. Locals were convinced she sold watered-down produce, but - suspected of being a witch - she went unchallenged. Cutting a lengthy story short – having finally been punished for doing so, Moll placed a curse upon the Castle. Legend has it she returned there in the guise of a mad black dog with fiery red eyes! Coaxed into the local river, the dog drowned. Any problems with mad dogs and any curses were now assumed to be over - but she returned - manifesting herself as – wait for it- 'a Grey Lady'. She remains in the property to this day, according to many.

Many a tourist has been followed around the Castle by Frances Greville – despite the fact she has long since been dead and buried. Footsteps of dead soldiers echo throughout the hallways and the pitiful wails from a desperate mother, who had been imprisoned with her child, have also been heard. HH & Spooky nights hold vigils at the Castle and you can book a suite on the Internet.

Coombe Abbey is another Warwickshire hotel, said to be haunted. I note a post on TripAdvisor in February 2020 from a fellow reviewer – who like me, wanted visitors to be aware of the fact of 'spectral activity'. Paranormal investigators booked a four day stay here in 2018 and fully intended to return in 2019 apparently - such was the abundance of activity. The lead investigator is quoted as saying they heard plenty of disembodied voices and ghostly footsteps – but the **'highlight'** of the stay was witnessing a chair move 2 ft across the room! They also thought themselves **'incredibly lucky'** to capture compelling evidence of a child (a deceased one obviously) which appeared on specialised SLS camera, in what was once the nursery. Good for them!

Aston Hall is a Jacobean House, located three miles north of Birmingham City Centre. It is home to at least four ghosts, the first being the daughter of Thomas Holte - not the nicest of chaps as it goes. Unhappy his daughter had no intention of marrying the man he deemed she should marry – he locked her in the attic - for sixteen years! She was driven to madness, which finally culminated in her death. She is seen in the upper floors – and is otherwise known as the *White Lady*. I can't help but think, they don't get terribly inventive with their names!

The second of our ghosts also haunting the property, is to be seen in the servants quarters. Legend has it, one night - less than happy with what had been served up for dinner - Thomas Holte took a hefty hatchet to the poor cook – splicing her head in two. Calling in a few favours, he escaped any charge for her murder. The third ghost is that of a young servant boy – Dick - accused by Thomas Holte of stealing food. Again, locked in a room awaiting a visit from his master, and dreading his punishment, he took his own life by hanging himself. He is seen in one of the upper floors.

The final ghost is the 'Green Lady', a former house-keeper of the property. She is most often seen downstairs.

As always, there are many more haunted abodes in and around Birmingham and the city runs ghost walks and tours.

I should finish by mentioning that Charles Dickens is said to haunt Birmingham Town Hall. Dickens gave his first reading of 'A Christmas Carol' here on Boxing Day 1853. Two workmen killed in an accident within the building are also said to haunt the premises.

Dickens was an avid investigator of the paranormal. Both he and Sir Arthur Conan Doyle were members of the infamous 'Ghost Club' founded in London in 1862. Other listed notable members include Mathematician Charles Babbage; Air Chief Marshall Lord Dowding; author Dennis Wheatley; actor Peter Cushing; Peter Underwood; life President of the Ghost Club and many other professional people, from all walks of life.

Their work is carried out on a scientific and logical basis - by means of a process of elimination initially. For example, having ruled out the obvious first i.e. If the lights reportedly switch on and off, or flicker of their own accord, the group check how 'sound' the electrics are in the property. If objects move on a regular basis, is the property prone to subsidence? I note they do not permit the use of Ouija boards within a property! Or at least they used not to. Sensible people that they are!

Some of the properties I have previously mentioned in this book that the club have investigated are *Ham House* (Richmond), the *Queen's House* (York) and the *Ram Inn* (Wootton-on-Edge). I see they have investigated one hotel local to me – the *Tontine Hotel*, Ironbridge in Shropshire. A later chapter reveals more of *The Tontine*, and those who still *'linger'* inside it.

Ettington Park Hotel
Ettington Park Hotel by Richard Croft, CC BY-SA 2.0,

Newman Brothers the Coffin Works Museum
Courtesy of Sarah Hayes

23

OUIJA BOARDS

THE ORIGINAL MANUFACTURER of the Talking or **Ouija** Board was the Kennard Novelty Company. Having found investors, a name was needed for the product. Recruiting the help of a medium, they decided to ask the board what it should be called - it spelt OUIJA. When they asked what that meant, it replied 'Good Luck'. Trust me - having heard and read some of the experiences of those who thought experimenting with a talking board would be a little fun, in many reported incidents, it turned out to be anything but that!

Hitting the market in 1891, the product was an instant success. The Victorians thought it extremely good - and more to the point - harmless fun, regularly bringing the board out for their after-dinner entertainment.

Many liken the Ouija Board to Pandora's Box, should it not be used correctly. One never knows what may be unleashed. These are the recommendations (not of my making - but of those *'in the know'*) should you choose to venture onto one.

1. *'Never use it whilst on your own'.*
2. *'Never use a Ouija Board in your own home'.*

I think it fair to say, there is absolutely no chance of me doing either! The next one sounds the most ominous...

3. *'If the spirit starts to count down, as in from 9 to 0, the numbers marked out on all boards - or to spell out the alphabet - end the session immediately! Placing the planchette on the word* **Goodbye** *(another sign displayed on any board) as you have inadvertently contacted a malevolent spirit!'* Great! This is also the case if it spells out the name **ZOZO**. Likewise end the session straight away!

4. *'Never use it in a cemetery'*. You would do well to get me in a cemetery at the best of times - let alone in the dark for a session on the old Ouija board!

5. *'Never burn the board!'* If you are having problems - it quotes - *'store the planchette and board separately'*. I wonder what problems they might be referring to - I dread to think.

6. *'Never ask a Ouija Board who, in the room, will die'*. Well, we're all going to die one day, are we not! Nevertheless, we'll respect any advice given.

7. *'Don't taunt or goad a spirit into speaking to you'*. No fear of that!

8. *'Don't joke, or jest'*. As far as I'm concerned, I don't find the meddling in such things the least bit funny.

I could go on - but by now - I think you will have got the gist, that these are dangerous things. They are not a toy, and not an innocent after dinner game. Stick to Charades or Monopoly.

Spirits may lay claim, via the board, to be a loved one or friend, but in effect, they are often malevolent strangers. You may, instead, find you have acquired an uninvited guest, who has every intention 'of sticking around for the foreseeable'- furthermore - one that means you harm. So, for goodness sake stay off the things!

Should I still not have dissuaded you from venturing onto a board, please abide by the rule book, and of course, 'GOOD LUCK'.

Just when I thought nothing else could leave me flabbergasted, I have discovered one edition of the board was manufactured in a pretty pink box - as a toy no less! as recently as 2009, by the giant toy company Hasbro. It was sold on Amazon. **What!** The Catholic Church and other Christian denominations have asked governments to ban the sale of them, claiming they are a doorway to demonic powers. I note there are none for sale currently on Amazon – and long may it stay that way!

Two friends of mine both describe the practice of engaging with an unidentified person on a board as truly terrifying. One tells me that no-one who was present on the night they went on the Ouija board, has ever spoken of the experience again, so alarming was it! Tony was 15 at the time - he is now 69. The memory still sends shivers down his spine.

I would like at this point to thank Christine Brown, who went to a great deal of trouble to relate the night when she also ventured onto such a board. This is her recollection of events.

"We were all in the kitchen of my friend's house in 54 Park Road, Walsall. The property was built on the land that once belonged to the wealthy Scott family.

Friends of the family had brought a Ouija Board, thinking it would be fun to try it out as my friend's father had said he kept hearing strange noises at night. Everyone was in a good mood and game for a bit of fun. It turned out to be anything but fun!

Mum and Dad went into the lounge, leaving seven youngsters in control of the board!

The first question was - *'IS THERE ANYBODY THERE?'*

The answer came back quickly with the glass whizzing round the letters - *'YES'*.

The second question - 'IS GRANDAD THERE?' (Grandad was very *'Yorkshire')*.

The answer came back – *'AYE LAD'*.

The third question – 'IS THERE A SPIRIT IN THE HOUSE?'

The glass was moving at a frenetic speed, so another questioned was asked - 'WHAT IS ITS NAME?'

The answer came back – 'PETER SCOTT'.

Next question – 'HOW DID HE DIE?'

Answer - 'IN A LAKE'.

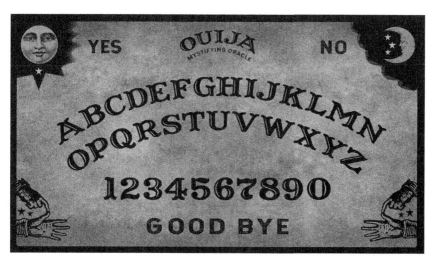

Kennard Toy Company Ouija Board
Attributed to Elijah Bond

On hearing the name Peter Scott, Mr Vincent came back into the room and stopped the session immediately. By this time everyone was very scared! The atmosphere was menacing in the extreme. I cannot emphasise enough the dangers of a Ouija Board."

It is, apparently, documented that Peter Scott did die in the lake. Peter and other members of his family were known to have practiced black magic, and because of this, are buried in unconsecrated ground in the grounds of the Scott Estate. I have been unable to verify if this is correct.

A housing estate has long since been built on this land, therefore, it does lead you to wonder if by any chance, any of its residents have any ghostly occupants?

24

ABANDON SHIP!

I HAVE JUST received a telephone call from a friend, which I think will be of interest. She has recently returned from a cruise on P & O's cruise ship 'Aurora'. Such was her enthusiasm to relate her tale about a fellow passenger, she could barely get the words out fast enough. Her fellow passenger was a lady, approximately 70 years of age, who was cruising alone. Having taken a photograph of herself in her cabin on her mobile phone, and then, duly sending it to her daughter, she was in immediate receipt of a reply.

'Who is the woman behind you?'

Our passenger's reply was that there was no one else with her - she was quite alone.
Her daughter responded with a further text

'There's a young woman behind you. There's a face. She looks Asian in origin - but the vision is blurred. See for yourself – you are not on your own!'

The lady looked at the photograph she had sent. Sure enough, it appeared she had a fellow cabin mate! Initially she showed the photograph to her fellow diners, who all heartily agreed, a young face could be seen behind her in the cabin. Not revealing the content of the photograph, the cabin boy was asked if anything untoward had happened in her cabin. Indeed, it had! Only a year ago, a Chinese girl had leapt from this balcony into the raging sea below. I may not have abandoned ship at this point, but I can categorically say, if the opportunity arose, I would have abandoned the cabin! Were that not possible, many nights would have been spent during the remainder of the cruise sleeping in one of the many steamer chairs on deck. I cursed my friend for not noting which cabin number it was.

THE ORIGINAL QUEEN MARY.

Permanently cast in the harbour at Long Beach, California, the cruise liner, RMS Queen Mary, is operating as a floating hotel, museum and tourist attraction. Built in the 1930s, it is an Art Deco delight. Cabin walls are lined in highly polished wooden veneers, with period furniture to complement the style. Intricate marquetry, marble, and glass décor is a sight to behold throughout the ship. Its mural artwork in public areas is simply stunning. It is exquisitely elegant - a living museum of opulence. It is also - home to many lost souls of the high seas!

Her decks have witnessed an astonishing number of deaths, be they in the form of accidental or deliberate acts. Converted during the war years, to carry troops, she collided with one of her escort ships, HMS Curacoa. 238 lives were lost in this accident alone. Given there are no less than 49 deaths recorded on this ship, some of which were murders, is it any wonder it possesses a plethora of hauntings! Each deck is said to be haunted. Cabin B430, having had a reputation for being a less than peaceful place to rest one's weary head, was finally taken out of service, when a member of staff was found murdered within it. The cabin (not before time) was deemed no longer suitable for guests. Even the number on the door has been removed!

Other cabins have also experienced odd disturbances. Passengers have woken to find a little boy standing beside the bed, staring blankly at them, before seeming to dissipate before their eyes. Taps turn on and off in the middle of the night, as do lights. Faces appear in mirrors that do not belong to anyone currently frequenting the cabin (well no living persons at least). Bed throws are reportedly tugged off by unseen hands.

Despite having long since passed away, Second Officer William Stark maintains a watch over the main deck. The Captain's steward accidently poured a glass of cleaning fluid, instead of one containing gin, and Stark - having drunk it - refused to have his stomach pumped, thinking it all a fuss over nothing. In a matter of days, on returning to Southampton, he was rushed to hospital, and within hours pronounced dead. His body was later returned to the ocean for a sea burial.

The swimming pools are still a popular congregational area for our spirit guests, despite the pools being empty of water for over 30 years now. The sound of splashing water is often heard and long since departed bathers have been seen in a range of swimwear fashions from the 1930s through to the 1960s.

John Pedder, an engineer on board the *Queen Mary*, was crushed in a freak accident in 1966. During a routine drill, the door of escape hatch (numbered 13) severed the poor chap in two. It is believed he was not the only person to have lost his life attempting to pass through door 13. An entire family, including a child, was murdered aboard the ship. She is seen and heard, in the cargo or second-class pool area, calling out for her mother. Another instance tells of an insane father who killed his five-year-old daughter whilst aboard the *Queen Mary*. Some think it is he who is the cause of the malice emanating from cabin B430.

Despite the risk of encountering these phantom nautical passengers, and the many more besides I have not mentioned, I, as a lover of all things 'Art Deco', would happily go on board - or at least I think I would? There are a variety of ghost tours available, which can be done independently or with guides. See the Internet for more details.

Our maiden cruise was taken on board the Queen Mary 2 - and it was splendid, the highlight being the sail into Venice at 7.30 in the morning. In order to take advantage of this extraordinary journey, we opted to eat breakfast on our cabin balcony. It was truly memorable. It had never occurred to us (but then why should it?) that the only means of transportation for anything and everything to and from Venice, would inevitably be by way of boat or barge. We watched a removal van moor up, followed by a juggernaut truck carrying fresh produce, but most notably, witnessed a lengthy funeral cortege sail through the canal. In true Venetian style, it was a spectacular sight. Resplendently decked out in wreaths, the coffin sat afloat a highly polished black gondola, its seats upholstered in black velvet. It was pure Venetian theatre. I cannot think of a more dramatic way to send loved ones to their final resting place, than by means of a gentle sail up the Grand Canal in a gondola, with a melodious yet still mournful tune played by a lone violinist to accompany them.

On that note, we'll take the opportunity to navigate the islands, canals and waterways of Venice ourselves, where the spookiest of spooky places await.

I have two young friends – aged 29 at the time – who, having been told of the places I have written about in this next chapter, couldn't wait to go on one of the ghost tours. On booking out, they asked the question – is the hotel haunted? The answer, as it is so often, a resounding yes! They were so pleased they hadn't known on arrival!

1st class Accommodation of Queen Mary
By User:Geographer, CC BY 2.5, https://common

25

MANY A MENACE IN VENICE

IN MY HUMBLE opinion, never was a city better suited to Hallowe'en than Venice. Throw into the pot the dense sea fogs, which, come Autumn, regularly smother the islands, and all that falls in its path, in a damp heavy mist. Inevitably - by a lack of visibility - consider then, the continual ominous blare from a ship's foghorn. Add to that, the sound of lapping water, the clank and creak of empty bobbing gondolas, and your own echoing footsteps as you walk abandoned canal alleyways come nightfall - quite alone - but are you?

The canals, the alleys, enveloped as they are by elongated shadows cast by the old buildings towering over them, are now cloaked in darkness.

Indubitably, Venetians are the strangest of folk to my mind! Liking nothing better than to stroll, incognito, using all manner of eerie masks to hide their identity. Furthermore, wearing the most flamboyant outrageous costumes, tricorn hats, capes and the weirdest of wigs, they remain intentionally mute, using mime as their means of communication. Frankly - it fair gives me the *heebie jeebies*!

The masks - to me - are downright sinister! Painted lips appear to sneer; the eyes - cut out slits, through which the wearer can peer at you - yet you in turn - have no idea as to the identity of the person behind the mask. More importantly, one is unable to determine what they (the wearer) might be thinking or intending to do! It really is quite menacing.

Venturing into the squares, where you naively think there will be safety in numbers, you happen upon human statues. Disconcerting (to me at least!) by their dead, yet strangely staring, searching eyes, you perceive them to be still - and then - in slow motion, they change their pose. I do wish they wouldn't do that - it's so creepy!

If I should bump into such masked revellers in the narrow alleyways in Venice known as the *Assassins* - well - heaven only knows what I may do? Scream - very loudly, probably!

Many murders have been committed in the alleyways, consequently they are rumoured to be haunted by numerous disgruntled victims, and who can blame them!

Yes - it has indeed - the perfect ingredients for an *'eerily elegant'*, yet decidedly menacing Hallowe'en. There is no need for a bat - punctured pumpkin – corpse, nor mummified body - the grisliest of grisly masks, neither hefty blood-stained cleaver in sight - nor the cackles of a mad witch. Merely unnaturally silent humans, dressed in the prettiest of masks will be enough to scare the hell out of most of us! And that's not forgetting the sound of that distant relentless foghorn!

The eeriest novels and short stories have been set in this city. Amongst them, *'Don't Look Now'* by Daphne du Maurier, brought to the cinema screen by Nicolas Roeg, Susan Hills' *'The Man in the Picture'*, and Henry James' *'The Aspen Papers'* to name but a few.

There are 118 islands in the lagoon. 400 bridges connect its dark cobbled narrow streets together. At the turn of each corner, another bridge awaits you; each street, it seems, a mirror image of the one before. From experience I know it is only too easy to get disorientated, hence, lost in the city.

As most Italians head off across the water at the end of a day's trading, it quite literally becomes a ghost town, save for the remaining tourists, hoteliers and restaurateurs working the nightshift.

Venice really does seem to have a rather macabre history. One of the most morbid places in Venice must surely be the *Island of Poveglia*. Initially the island was used as a mass incineration and burial site for those having contracted bubonic plague. The disease was spread by the fleas living on rats – *urgh*! Perish the thought! Any Venetians suspected of carrying the disease, were deposited upon the island and left to die. Later the island was used for the same purpose, segregating victims of the Black Death. Both plagues were spread by fleas. If that were not horrid enough, the 1920s saw a mental institution constructed here, run by an unscrupulous doctor. Supposedly in the name of science, he tortured many mentally ill patients, using bizarre and horrendous therapies. He later committed suicide - throwing himself from the bell tower. He was supposedly driven to it by the ghosts inhabiting the island. Serves him jolly well right!

The hospital and crematorium remain. No one is permitted on the island without prior permission from the Government. Frankly I have no idea why anyone would want to go anyway.

The precise number of bodies laid to rest here is hard to determine, but it is believed there are some 160,000 skeletons scattered in open graves.

Many a person sailing past the island, speaks of hearing agonizing wails and distraught cries for help. Is it any wonder?

In 2014 the Italian state announced it would grant a 99-year lease for redeveloping the island into a luxurious hotel complex. Heavens above! I cannot think of anywhere I would be less likely to choose to visit as a holiday destination. After an outcry from locals the idea has been shelved – for now at least.

Casin dei Spiriti (House of the Spirits) is haunted by the ghost of a former inhabitant who committed suicide within the property. It was also the scene of a grisly murder that took place in the 1950s. The victim was a young lady, whose body was cut into pieces and then disposed of into the water. Fishermen still refuse to fish there - is it pray - any wonder? Imagine finding a finger or a toe on the end of the line. It is located near the Rialto Bridge, and room reservations are available. Putting gruesome tales to one side, it does appear to be a very nice place to stay. As always it can be located on the Internet.

Sailing on the Grand Canal you come upon a palace known by locals as '*The House of No Return*'. Fifteen of the Ca Dario inhabitants have died in suspicious circumstances. Five more went bankrupt, and three met with serious accidents. Other than that, the place is good to go.

The island of *Lazzaretto Nuovo* (reached from stop number 13) is another mass burial site. The skeleton of a woman was found on the island, with a brick wedged in her mouth. This gave rise to assume the woman had been suspected of being a 'Shroud Eater' (a type of vampire) who liked nothing better than to chew on the dead! Obviously, a brick was considered as a good a tool as any to deal with the problem.

Progressing further we head to the *Island of the Mad* (Isola del Pazzo). Operating from 1795 as a mental asylum, it was run by monks. 1978 saw its closure as an asylum. Strangely enough it was reopened in 2006, serving as a small museum, commemorating its former use as a psychiatric hospital. Equipment remains intact, together with photographs of former patients on view. I can't help but think it a strange thing to want to see, but perhaps it's me?

For any avid 'ghostbuster' the ghost tours are a must to do whilst in Venice. Many include a ride on a gondola as part of the tour.

You might also want to avoid the Venice carnival dates as well if you are not keen on masks. The fear of masks is known as 'Maskaphobia'.

Venetians were originally only permitted to wear masks between St. Stephen's Day (26th December) up to and including the carnival season. They were also permitted to be worn in celebration of the feast of Ascension, and finally from 5th October until Christmas. Seemingly Venetians gain a great deal of pleasure from being 'masked up'.

The use of the masks was forbidden in 1797 under the rule of the King of Austria.

Seeing a pretty penny to be made, they were revived in a big way in 1979 by the Italian government bringing back the carnival.

The *Dottore Peste* mask is immediately recognisable by its large beaked nose. It has an opening for the eyes and a scarf over the face. The mask was worn by doctors, visiting the plague victims. Spices and herbs were carried in the beak in an attempt to purify the air from the stench of diseased bodies and that of the dead. On that cheerful note I think that's enough on the tales of Venice and its multitude of dead bodies. So let's head instead to the fair…

Venice Carnival
Courtesy of Markus Donner
Pixabay

Venice Carnival
Courtesy of Markus Donner
Pixabay

26

ALL THE FUN OF THE FAIR

THINGS GET NO more thrilling than at the fairground - especially when you throw a few ghosts into the mix! The world's first ghost train was erected in Blackpool Pleasure Beach in 1936, and yes, you guessed correctly - it's haunted! An attentive former maintenance worker on the ride is the phantom haunting the train. He is nicknamed 'Cloggy' thanks to his choice of shoe attire. Cloggy passed away in 1970. Following his demise, passengers complained of being physically touched whilst aboard the ghost train. Subsequently they discovered, to their horror, that they were at the mercy of a ghostly hand, not as they thought, by a current employee operating the ride. I am not sure which repulses me more, a living hand manhandling me, or a dead one?

The North Pier Blackpool is home to at least three ghosts. One - a rather romantic story - involves a middle aged Victorian lady. Wearing a long grey skirt, short jacket and hat, she carries a parasol (I am reminded of Mary Poppins) and is regularly seen in several places; at the pier entrance, where she likes nothing better than to take a ride on the carousel. She is also seen sitting on a bench, from which she rises, then to glide down the pier, and disappear. She has also been spied passing her time in the Sun Lounge.

Mary Poppins was the fictional nanny conjured up by P.L.Travers. The character was later brought to the film screen by Walt Disney, and - it would seem - *Disneyland* itself is swarming with ghosts, including *Walt Disney* himself!

One ghost, known as '*Mr One Way*', rides upon '*Space Mountain*'. He has a tendency to travel with lone passengers - even to interact with them - but never completes the trip. A second ghost, named '*Disco Debbie*' is seen as a fluorescent green light. I'm not entirely sure how you could differentiate a fluorescent green light from any other of the flashing neon lights in a fairground – but who am I to spoil a good tale.

'Disco Debbie' (Deborah Gail Stone) worked as a performer at Disneyland. Involved in a dreadful freak accident, she died during a performance. Unbeknown to fellow cast members at the time it happened, she was crushed between a stationary and moving set. It wasn't until sometime later that her body was found. People had heard screams, but thought it part of the show.

Bizarrely, many people try to sneak their deceased loved ones ashes into Disneyland's *'Haunted Mansion'*, some having succeeded over the course of time. Alarmingly, one mother deposited her child's ashes in there! What was the woman thinking of! Poor little mite! The child, it appears, isn't as keen on the idea of being abandoned in a haunted mansion. I can't for the life of me think why not! It is he, many suspect, who is heard sobbing inside. Having been in the Haunted House myself, I don't blame the poor little soul! My recollection of events varies according to what I see and read of it nowadays.

Apparently nowadays the experience begins nothing like this. I entered a room first, in which was stood a severe looking woman dressed in a 1920-30s' maid's outfit. Having been gathered in, the walls began to move inwards, pushing us all closer together. The first thing that occurred to me was, what if the mechanism is faulty? We're going to be crushed!

The boy is by no means the only ghost to reside in the Haunted Mansion. There is a phantom gent in a tuxedo, who so frightened one worker by laying his hand on her shoulder, that she quit the job there and then. Nor is she the only person to have done so.

One male passenger in the 'Haunted Mansion' was so scared by the whole experience that he suffered a heart attack, and died!

A teenager travelling the 'Haunted Mansion' ride, leapt from his car, missed the platform on to which he should have landed, fell 15 foot, and died having broken his neck. There have in fact, been an extraordinary number of accidents since Disneyland opened in 1955. One cannot help but wonder, how often are injury claims settled out of court?

A cheerier tale to be told, is that of a kindly lady lingering on *Main Street*. Dressed in 19th century white attire, she has been known to help lost children to the child collection area. This kindly spirit is thought to have lived on the site before it was re-developed.

Many maintenance crews dread checking the rides at the end of the day, having experienced all manner of unusual happenings. As always, a number of people, taking unnecessary risks, have died on the rides. Dolly Young was one example, for, in 1989 she met her end in a very gruesome way on *'The Matterhorn'*. Bizarrely, she undid her restraining strap for reasons we will never know; you can guess the rest. Her voice is heard by staff members when inspecting the rides at the end of the day.

Those dastardly dolls rear their demon heads yet again in Disneyland of all places, in what is known as *'It's a Small World'*. Some of the animatronic figures spring to life, despite the power to them being switched off. *'Darn those damned dolls'* I say! Workers also report lights being flicked on and off, and the sound of tiny footsteps and giggling, when the ride is closed and all the equipment switched off. Thank god I never knew that when I went on it!

Along with our 'ghostly energised dolls' the puppets and props within *'Pirates of the Caribbean'* have been seen to move of their own volition - without need of electronics to help them on their merry way. Sometimes they even up-sticks – and move considerable distances.

To impart some authenticity to the ride, real skeletal bones were originally used to decorate the sets. The majority have now been replaced. Those whose bones still remain housed within, appear perhaps, not particularly happy to be there!

Maintenance crews also report seeing a ghostly boy on CCTV, who regularly enjoys this particular ride.

I haven't revealed all the extraordinary accidental deaths in Disneyland, as I said, there are so many! But a final one is that of Thomas Cleveland. In 1966 his life came to a somewhat horrifying end, when trying to access the park free of charge via the monorail. His end was a messy one, as he was sucked into the mechanism. His ghost is seen walking the monorail track late at night.

I could go on, for there is an abundance of spirits to be witnessed at Disneyland California. We might well have known America would do hauntings bigger and better than anyone else, yet, fear not, Britain is not without its own haunted theme park. One located smack bang right in the centre of England, and unlike Disneyland's Haunted House, ours is an authentic property.

Alton Towers is a well-known theme resort located in Staffordshire. The current house, the last to be built on the site of a former country house estate, was completed in 1850. This once stately home has long since stood derelict, yet its interior is still in frequent use.

Many internal fixtures, along with its lead roofing, were sold off. Consequently, rain water seeped in, and the house soon fell into disrepair. However, its dilapidated state, somehow adds to its appeal (to some at least) as a haunted property worth attending a one night ghostly vigil in. And it is apparently, teeming with spirits! Check out the HH & Spooky Nights website should you wish to buy tickets.

The ghost most often seen strolling the corridors is that of a lady in a long dark dress - and it seems the scent of her perfume wafts in the air. Despite a no smoking rule, the odour of stale cigar smoke in other parts of the mansion is sometimes perceived. Doors are both heard and seen slamming shut, and cackles come aplenty from the kitchen. Despite a lack of furniture, dragging sounds are other alarming noises often heard. Orbs are picked up on photographs, as well as seen with the naked eye. I have to say I'm sceptical, this is a fairground at the end of the day.

You may encounter a large man around the music room area. Also, the sound of his footsteps have been heard also in the Banqueting Hall. When the 'Most Haunted' team investigated the building in 2007, they picked up on a large hooded man, who was, to say the least, very aggressive. You can (as is often the case) always watch the visit on YouTube.

Incorporated, as the 'Hex' ride is, into the fabric of the building, partly into the mansion's old armoury and picture gallery, it fits perfectly into this Gothic revival architecture. Queuing for a go on the 'Hex' - tourists are often oblivious of the fact that they might well be pelted with stones and other objects, as they are standing in direct firing line of some apparition, who gains great pleasure from throwing things. Ghostly children dressed in Victorian clothes have been seen. Is it them perhaps, who are the culprits?

The ride is based upon the true tale of the chained oak tree, which still stands in the grounds. The house and grounds were cursed by an old beggar woman who had once stopped the 15th Earl of Shrewsbury to ask for money. Foolishly, he ignored her. Having been refused a charitable penny, she swore that each time a branch fell off the mighty oak, a death would occur in the family. That same night, amid an almighty thunder and lightning storm, an unexpected death in the family did occur. It was enough to convince the Earl this was no coincidence. In a vain attempt to ensure it never happened again, servants were ordered to chain every branch to the tree. It remains chained, and is visible for all to see. The theme of the 'Hex' ride is based on this cursed tale.

27

WHAT IS IT WITH CRICKET?

HAVING TOLD YOU of Stuart Broad's nightly 'visitation' at The Langham, it would be remiss of me to fail to mention the ghostly tales other international cricket teams have also experienced. They all occurred in one hotel, the *Lumley Castle, Durham*. Originally a manor house, it was converted into a Castle in 1389.

It looms large over the Chester le Street cricket ground.

It is renowned – predominantly - for being haunted by Lily of Lumley, the secret wife (for a while at least) of Sir Ralph Lumley.

Having married a Catholic, Lily refused to convert to the Catholic faith, and was duly murdered by two priests, who later disposed of her body, by throwing it down the Castle well.

So unnerved were three members of the visiting 2001 West Indies cricket team, they opted to check out of the hotel in the middle of the night. 'Duppy Conquerors' (Jamaican lingo for ghost conquerors) they were not! Their reason for having left in such haste remains unanswered.

Sourav Ganguly had a similar experience to that of Stuart Broad back at The Langham, in that the taps in his room kept turning themselves on and off - when likewise - he switched the light by his bed on and off. Abandoning his room, he asked Robin Singh if he might sleep on the floor of his room instead.

Petrified of the place, Rahul Dravid asked his team director in 2011 whether they were to be staying at the *Lumley Castle Hotel* again. He was exceptionally relieved to hear they were not. Actually, the Indian team never returned, opting instead to stay a good deal further from the Durham ground than might be deemed practical.

During the 2005 Ashes tour, the Australian cricket team also stayed at the Lumley Castle Hotel. Stories vary as to what Shane Watson, aged 24 at the time, actually experienced.

Figuring there is safety to be had in numbers, he opted to abandon his room in the middle of the night, sleeping instead on the floor of Brett Lee's.

After much barracking on the pitch the following day from Darren Gough, an alternative room was offered to Watson. Much relieved, he moved into room 46. What he didn't know was, that was the same room in which Lily was murdered!

The heckling by Gough can be viewed on YouTube, it is hilariously funny.

Other spirits linger longer than many might like them to, within the castle. Despite there being no children in situ at the time, they have been heard running and squealing in rooms on the top floor.

Black Jack is another otherworldly spirit. Somewhat of a prankster, he gains a great deal of pleasure in hiding guests items, whilst also knocking glasses off tables.

One final ghost is that of a gent who appears sitting at the bar, who then slowly dissipates before your eyes.

Manchester United football team have also stayed there. No one left before daybreak, but neither have they ever returned.

Paul Collingwood and his wife left their room in the middle of the night, so unnerved by the eerie ambience of the place. It does make you wonder, does it not, what it is about it, that spooks people out?

Should a visit appeal to you, Lumley Castle Hotel also advertise *'Escape Room'* experiences team@escapedurham.co.uk. The reviews at the time of writing (there being three themes to choose from) are excellent. One features the Lily of Lumley experience.

28

IS THERE ANYBODY THERE?

Courtesy of Olivia Flemming Smith

THROUGH THE EXPERIENCES of a young friend, one who, without wishing to sound too melodramatic, seems to attract the attentions of those from the 'other side', I can reveal two more hotels that might be of interest to those who do wish to visit a haunted property. My young friend's name is Olivia. She is an operatic crossover singer. Her profession regularly takes her to hotels and historic buildings. Like me, she isn't keen to experience 'otherworldly things' - but doesn't seem to have a great deal of choice in the matter. Having been booked for an evening performance, Olivia arrived at the *Shrigley Hall Hotel*, blissfully unaware that it is listed as one of the most haunted hotels in England. There is no known background to whoever it is, but this ghost is keen to put in regular appearances.

The original owners were the De Shrigley's. The MP William Turner purchased the estate in 1818. By 1825 the Hall was completely re-constructed. In 1827, Turner's daughter, 15 year-old Ellen (sole heiress), was abducted from her school by Gibbon Wakefield, a 30 year-old British diplomat. Lured away under false pretences, she was tricked into marrying Wakefield at Gretna Green. Fortunately for Ellen, she was rescued en route to Calais by her uncle. The marriage was annulled two years later by Parliament. Ellen - having married again - died in childbirth. She was only 19 years old.

In 1929 the *Salesians order* purchased Shrigley Hall, converting it into a missionary college. In 1936 they added a chapel to the south wing. Programmed to perform in the *Salesians Chapel*, otherwise known as the *Tilden Suite*, Olivia was allocated *The Chapel Room*, in which to change and leave any belongings. This was accessed by a staircase leading onto a landing.

As a professional singer she headed off to a quieter area (or so she thought!) to prepare. Standing in a dark room, in front of a large golden mirror, Olivia noticed to her right, two open wooden doors. From the room to which the doors led, there came a sudden loud insistent clanging noise. It seemed, to Olivia, to be that of metal banging on pipework. At the same time, Olivia felt a draft passing across her. It was at this point she felt someone was watching her.

'Straight away, I knew it was a ghost - and then I thought of you!' she said.

Not wishing to cause a commotion, vocal exercises were promptly abandoned. The show would go on, but without any warm up exercises! I should mention there was no sign of anyone in the adjacent room. She was quite on her own. Unfortunately for Olivia there was yet another costume change to be made, which entailed one more visit to the dreaded 'landing'. Once up there, choosing a different location that might prove less 'stressful', she opted this time to turn left, where she came upon a wrought iron spiral stairway.

'It did look a bit spooky' she said.

In the midst of her costume change, the sound of reverberating metal, was heard again.

'It sounded like approaching footsteps upon the metal stairs' .

Both she and her sister heard it. Both expected someone to appear at the top of the spiral staircase - nobody however, did. As is so often the case in such a situation, they both began to laugh. A little hysterically I should imagine. They had no idea why they did so, for it was no laughing matter. The bar staff later related that no-one is keen to venture down into the cellars of this Hotel.

Shrigley Hall Hotel is exquisitely elegant. Located on the edge of the Peak district, it is a beautiful place to visit. It can be found on the *Most Haunted Hotels* website and on its own website.

Progressing to her next encounter, heading in a north westerly direction, Olivia became a resident for three nights at *Irton Hall Hotel*, Holmrook - where within - yet another *Grey Lady* makes the odd appearance. Not that Olivia was aware of this at the time! At least on this occasion, Harry her boyfriend was in situ. Harry also admits to hearing the commotion that woke them both, on the second night, at 3am. The noise was that of furniture being moved in the room above. It went on for about ten minutes, and then a second time for approximately three.

'It was not a slow dragging screech; it was more as if the furniture was being dragged at great speed! I thought at the time, why on earth would anyone move furniture around at such early hours?'

The following morning she went outside. Looking up, she realised, to her horror - there was no room above theirs. At least, what roof space there was, would not be large enough to encompass furniture and a person capable of moving furniture within it. Heading off to reception, she asked the usual question, receiving the dreaded answer. She was informed there was a ghost in the attic, directly above her room. The receptionist echoed without prompting, that the sound of furniture being moved, is heard. Interestingly, Irton is 'dog friendly', therefore I do wonder if the dogs ever sense anything. Postings on TripAdvisor might be of use?

Irton Hall was visited by both Oliver Cromwell and Henry the sixth. Henry, as a Lancastrian, was refused shelter at Irton Hall by its *Yorkist* owner. However, his wife, Anne Irton, secretly helped the king find sanctuary, and in turn paid a hefty price for it! Having discovered her treachery, her husband had her locked in Pele tower, where, in turn, she was starved to death. Her ghost is known as 'The Grey Lady'. You can view Pele Tower on YouTube. It is available as self-catering accommodation. You can still ascend the spiral stone steps up to the room she was imprisoned in.

Olivia, like me, seems to attract spirits like a 'moth to a flame'. She is also about as brave as me - which is 'not very brave at all!'.

29

THE TONTINE HOTEL & RAF COSFORD

SET AMID WOODLAND, erected on a steep incline that leads down to the River Severn, are an eclectic mixture of properties.

There are Georgian houses - some five and six storeys high. Access is gained to them by way of steep winding narrow lanes.

In the centre of Ironbridge itself, brick-laid alleyways lead you to the quaint 18th century workers' cottages, scattered randomly (or so it feels) here and there. These properties would have housed local foundry workers, and other manual labourers.

Then there are the impressive Victorian villas, elaborately finished in coloured bricks, iron balustrades', and decorative tiles manufactured down river in nearby Jackfield.

It's hard to imagine this idyllic tourist 'hot-spot' was once the epicentre of the Industrial Revolution, the air then, polluted with acrid smoke emitted from the blast furnaces. Everything in the surrounding area, continually covered in a grimy black dust. The area - rich in sandstone and clay, explains the existence of the bottle kilns – still seen today, their ovens fired by the coal which was also mined nearby.

The Tontine Hotel
Courtesy of Russ Taylor

The *Ironbridge Gorge* is a UNESCO World Heritage site. The whole area is steeped in history, and I know for a fact that many of its public hostelries and other buildings are said to be haunted.

The Tontine Hotel is our focal point. The hotel was built in such a position as to have the prime vantage point from which to view the world's first iron bridge. It is one to have been investigated by the prestigious *'Ghost Club'*. I am aware of only one other place in Shropshire to have been granted a nightly vigil by the group – RAF Cosford - though of course, should that not be the case I stand corrected!

The Tontine Hotel experiences a multitude of disturbances and ghostly activity in the bar area - the cellars - even the living quarters of the hoteliers - but most importantly perhaps, to you and me - its guests' rooms, one of those being room 5. On the 6th September 1950, Frank Griffin murdered Jane Edge, landlady of the Queens' Head, Ketley. Having committed the murder, he fled to the Tontine Hotel, he went into hiding in that very room. However, he was found, arrested and tried for the murder. He was imprisoned in Shrewsbury Prison, where he was executed, on the 4th January 1951.

Room 5 experiences bathroom taps being turned on by some unseen presence. Orbs have been caught on camera. The usual inexplicable cold temperature drops, are often experienced – but perhaps most intriguingly, timepieces have been reported as proceeding to suddenly work in an anti-clockwise motion! Some reckon it's Frank's attempt to gain himself more time to escape.

Digressing for a moment, I would explain at this point, that there are three types of hauntings. The first - **Residual Type Hauntings**. These are likened to watching a film replay of an event, occurring time and time again. These spirits don't interact with the living - they are just visible to us. They often don't realise they are in fact - dead.

The second are **Intelligent Type Hauntings**. The ghost attempts to interact with – and - on occasions – is able to communicate with the living. He or she, will try to communicate either by touching people, or by moving objects. And of course, by making themselves visible. Emitting an odour, and making the living hear something, are two other ways of attracting attention. Interestingly, the only one of our senses not affected is that of taste, although, in all manner of places, people sensitive to a visitation are prone to feeling nauseous.

This, on occasions, is experienced at The Tontine, in Room 9. If, having failed to achieve a line of communication by any of the previously named means, they may affect electrics and water (sources of natural energy).

There is a worrying aspect - and I stress at this point - that this is NOT the case at the Tontine - occasionally when timepieces and objects rotate regularly in an anticlockwise manner – it can be a third type of haunting - a *'Demonic Type Haunting'*. The Tontine has **no** dreadful entity such as this (thank goodness!) but people have felt an intimidating presence.

Some may scoff – but – to my mind at least, most will not deny the power of good, and countering that, the existence of an evil influence. Other telling signs that an evil entity is at work, is an accompanying strong offensive odour, and the presence of an apparition with either no eyes or reddish ones!

Yes – I know this all sounds very far-fetched! But many a church has been called upon to help with such problems, and they in turn take the matter very seriously, performing exorcisms.

It should be remembered, visitors who experienced such things at the Tontine, as at so many other places I have mentioned en route, were unaware the place was haunted. Importantly - they all describe the same experience, with no prior knowledge of what has been witnessed previously.

Peter Underwood (Life President of the Ghost Club) once said...

'We rely in court, on a person's word of an account of events - why should we doubt them at any other time.'

I would further add, we rely upon an honest account of events, whereby many swear on a Bible. These citizens faithfully believe in God - but has anyone ever actually seen God? Not as far as I am aware. And yet - I would neither wish to offend - nor insult anyone by claiming there was no such being, simply because I myself, have never seen him!

All that said, Room 9 is also an 'active' room. Guests have found it more disconcerting than any other to stay in. Even some of the hardened Ghost Club members who visited back in 2005, found it an uncomfortable place to remain in.

One hotel guest insisted he felt something had tried to strangle him! A number of guests, feeling ill at ease in a variety of rooms, have left prematurely - including one staying in Room 4, who swore the room went icy cold, just before he felt somebody sit down on the end of his bed! He couldn't see anybody, yet he could see an indentation on the bedcover and mattress! He sped from his bed, spending the rest of the night elsewhere, with his travelling companion.

Members of the *St. Milburga Lodge*, the clandestine institution most often referred to as *The Masons*, met regularly at the hotel until 1966. Visiting mediums sense a murder took place here that involved this enigmatic group.

With 10 museums to visit in Ironbridge, it is well worth a visit.

Whilst staying at the Tontine you may well wish to include a trip to *RAF Cosford*, where you will find a haunted *Avro Lincoln Bomber* RF398.

Fearing the aircraft was to be moved to Manchester, workers made up stories about the plane being haunted. However – the plan backfired when inexplicable things started to occur within the aircraft. Time to call in the experts!

Having sealed, securely, both the hangar and the plane entrances with signed masking tape, a variety of recording equipment was placed in the aircraft. The first time this was done, the investigators found, to their astonishment, on returning to the Bomber, that the lid of the cassette recorder had been flipped open, and the tape removed. Further recordings, on a variety of machines, revealed other noises. Having had the recordings tested for tampering (though no-one present quite knew how this could have happened) and eliminating radio waves that may have interfered with the noises heard, ex Lincoln Bomber pilots were sought. They recognised the sounds as those of working equipment within the plane. This aircraft's engines however, had been out of service since 1956!

Many have seen and felt the presence of an airman in the Bomber. He is assumed to be Master Pilot Hiller. Hiller, the last person listed as having flown the aircraft. Hiller died in an air crash not far from RAF Cosford. He is quoted as saying he loved his Lincoln. It was his baby – and swore he would haunt it.

On one occasion the BBC came to film a vigil. Larking around, they weren't taking things terribly seriously – that was - until their camera was picked up by some unknown presence and literally flung across the hangar. No-one was anywhere near the camera at the time. Petrified, they left immediately!

Watch Mark Felton's YouTube film, if you wish to view the plane, hear more tales of its ghostly pilot – and intriguingly – hear the sounds themselves.

Having visited Cosford on many occasions, I have to say, it is a sobering thought, that the thing that chills me more than most, is the sight of the Nazis' arsenal of weapons, which are terrifying by their size and what they may have achieved.

EPILOGUE

OBVIOUSLY, I AM unable to guarantee that you will encounter any of our spirit friends on your future journeys. However, having highlighted the places mentioned, hopefully I will have increased your chances of doing so.

Our braver friends will undoubtedly be revving the car engine up with the greatest alacrity, even as I type, and I wish them the best of luck in their pursuit of seeing otherworldly folk.

On the other hand, however fascinating some may have found the tales, if you are anything like me, you may have already disabled the satellite navigation system to any of the destinations aforementioned.

To increase your chances of seeing anything, choosing to visit when the property or area is less than busy, will indubitably help you. Dusk until dawn, are more often favourable times in which to witness things.

Your trip will have been in vain if you have noisy fellow travellers in tow. Leave any shrieking, hysterical and giggling passengers at home.

Should you be lucky (or unlucky) enough, dependent upon your view of the subject, to experience anything out of the ordinary, remember, be respectful, just as you would be to any living person.

Finally I wish you good luck, have a safe journey, and remember – resist any temptation to purchase any dolls or Ouija boards from any car boot sale, or antique shops you may call into en route home! And remember 'DO NOT DISTURB' are three words, on the odd occasion, well worth abiding by.

YOUR TRAVELLING COMPANION

ON THE FACE of it, I do seem susceptible to strange occurrences. I have never actually seen a ghost, a spirit (whichever it is you prefer to call them) yet I have undoubtedly experienced them. If a building or place is haunted, I am left in no doubt, that any manifestation will make its presence known to me. My family always say 'It always seems to happen to you'. It does, and I would much prefer it didn't!

Innocently perusing the shelves of Holland and Barrett one day, deliberating over which vitamin or mineral was going to do the most wonderous things for my state of health, I suddenly heard someone whistling the most extraordinarily irritating tune in my ear, which I found more than a little annoying! Turning to see who it was, I encountered no one. I expected to see a man (I have no idea why?). I looked down both aisles. There was no one there. Glancing at the till area, I saw that it was empty. I circumnavigated the entire shop. Not a soul anywhere. Well not a living one at least! Yet, I knew what I had heard. I had not imagined it.

I won't say I was afraid, more that I was flummoxed. Was someone playing a trick? I left, intrigued. Curiosity getting the better of me, I returned a week later. Waiting until the shop was empty, importantly, not revealing what I had experienced, I asked if the shop was haunted. The answer was yes! By a man, who liked nothing more than to sing or whistle unrecognisable tunes. Well I'll be damned!

≈

LIST OF HAUNTED PROPERTIES AND PLACES.

Carmarthenshire
Newton House

Cheshire
Tatton Old Park
Shrigley Hall Hotel

Cornwall
Prideux Place
Jamaica Inn

Cumbria
Irton Hall
Capesthorne Hall Hotel

Devon
Buckland Abbey
Buckfastleigh Caves

Hampshire
Spitbank Fort

Gloucestershire
Ram Inn

Isle of Wight
Lilliput Doll & Toy Museum
Ventnor Botanic Gardens
Appuldurcombe House
St Catherine's Lighthouse

Kent
Fan Bay Shelter
Chartwell

Lancashire
Blackpool Pleasure Beach

Liverpool
Newsham Park Hospital.
Speke Hall

London
The Langham
Georgian House Hotel
Grange Blooms Hotel
Ham House (Richmond)
50 Berkeley Square
The Royal Albert Hall
Her Majesty's Theatre London
Theatre Royal Drury Lane
The Palace Theatre
The Fortune Theatre
The National Maritime Museum
V & A Museum (Dolls)
All Saints church Livermere Rd.
Museum of Curiosities.
Highgate Cemetery

Norfolk
Felbrigg Hall

Powys
Powis Castle

Shropshire
Shrewsbury Prison
Shrewsbury Castle
Prince Rupert Hotel
The Lion Hotel
The Nag's Head Pub
The Feathers Hotel
The Globe Inn
The Blue Boar Inn
The Bull Hotel
Ludlow Castle
Ratlinghope
The Tontine Hotel
RAF Cosford

Somerset
Doll Museum
Dunster Castle

Staffordshire
Alton Towers

Warwickshire
Baddesley Clinton
New Street Station
Catacombs Warstone Lane
Cemetery
The Coffin Works Jewellery
Quarter
Alexandra Theatre B.ham
Steelhouse Lane Police Station
Ettington Park Hotel
Warwick Castle
Coombe Abbey Hotel
Aston Hall

Birmingham Town Hall

Worcestershire
Drakelow Tunnels

Yorkshire
Unicorn Hotel
Nunnington Hall
Ripon Workhouse & Prison
Treasurer's House York
Fountains Abbey.

FURTHER AFIELD

Austria
Hohensalszburg Castle Salzburg

California
Disneyland Long Beach
Queen Mary Liner Long Beach

Italy
Stresa
Rocca Di Angera Puppet Museum

Venice
Island of Povelgia
Casin dei Spiriti
Island of Lazzaretto Nuovo
Island of the Mad (Isola Del
Pazzo)

REFERENCES FOR WEBSITES

Royal Museum Greenwich
https://www.visitbritain.com Britain-most-haunted - hotels
https://www.hauntedrooms.co.uk/haunted-hotels/england
hauntedisland.co.uk
https//www.shrewsburyprison.com/ghosttours
https://nationaltrust.org.uk
Irton Hall Hotel
Martin Wood Haunted Shrewsbury
Prince Rupert Hotel
Gilly Pickup Author
Lilliput Doll Museum Isle of Wight
HH & Spooky Nights
Drakelow-tunnels.co.uk
Haunted Highgate Della Farrant
Spookyisles.com

Printed in Great Britain
by Amazon

56627370R00078